GRAMMAR AND BEYOND

Teacher Support Resource Book
with CD-ROM

Paul Carne

Jenni Currie Santamaria

Lisa Varandani

3

CAMBRIDGE
UNIVERSITY PRESS

CAMBRIDGE UNIVERSITY PRESS
Cambridge, New York, Melbourne, Madrid, Cape Town,
Singapore, São Paulo, Delhi, Tokyo, Mexico City

Cambridge University Press
32 Avenue of the Americas, New York, NY 10013-2473, USA

www.cambridge.org
Information on this title: www.cambridge.org/9781107685024

© Cambridge University Press 2012

First published 2012
2nd printing, 2012

Printed in the United States of America

A catalog record for this publication is available from the British Library.

ISBN 978-0-521-14298-4   Student's Book 3
ISBN 978-0-521-14315-8   Student's Book 3A
ISBN 978-0-521-14319-6   Student's Book 3B
ISBN 978-1-107-60197-0   Workbook 3
ISBN 978-1-107-60198-7   Workbook 3A
ISBN 978-1-107-60199-4   Workbook 3B
ISBN 978-1-107-68502-4   Teacher Support Resource Book with CD-ROM 3
ISBN 978-0-521-14339-4   Class Audio CD 3
ISBN 978-1-139-06187-2   Writing Skills Interactive 3

Art direction and layout services: Integra

Contents

Introduction

Grammar and Beyond is a four-level grammar series for beginning- to advanced-level students of North American English. The series focuses on the most commonly used grammar structures and includes a special emphasis on the application of these structures in academic writing. There is also a special focus on authentic language use in communicative contexts.

A Unique Approach

Grammar

The grammar presented is strongly informed by the *Cambridge International Corpus*. This corpus was created from the research and analysis of over one billion words of authentic written and spoken language data gathered from college lectures, textbooks, academic essays, high school classrooms, and conversations between instructors and students. By using the *Cambridge International Corpus*, the series contributors were able to:

- Present grammar rules that reflect actual North American English.
- Describe differences between the grammar of written and spoken English.
- Focus more attention on the structures that are commonly used, and less on those that are rarely used, in both written and spoken language.

Academic Writing Skills

The structure of *Grammar and Beyond* is designed to help students make the transition from simply understanding grammar structures to actually using them accurately in writing.

Error Avoidance

Each Student's Book unit features an *Avoid Common Mistakes* section that develops awareness of the most common mistakes made by English language learners and provides practice in detecting and correcting these errors. The mistakes highlighted in this section are drawn from the *Cambridge Learner Corpus*, a database of over 135,000 essays written by non-native speakers of English.

Vocabulary

Every unit in *Grammar and Beyond* includes words from the Academic Word List (AWL), a research-based list of words and word families that appear with high frequency in academic texts. These words are introduced in the opening text of the unit, recycled in the charts and exercises, and used to support the theme throughout the unit. The same vocabulary is reviewed and practiced in the corresponding unit of *Writing Skills Interactive*.

Instructional Resources

Teacher Support Resource Book with CD-ROM

In addition to an audio script and answer key for the Student's Book, this book contains general teaching suggestions for applying any of the structures taught in the Student's Book to all four major skill areas.

The CD-ROM in the back of the book includes:

PowerPoint Presentations

- Twenty-eight animated presentations offer unit-specific grammar lessons for classroom use. Their purpose is to provide engaging visual aids to help clarify complex grammatical concepts while encouraging a high level of student involvement.

Unit Tests

- Each of the 28 ready-made unit tests consists of two parts. Part I tests the grammar points in the order presented in the unit. Part II offers a more challenging blend of the grammar. Each unit test is easy to score on a scale of 100 points by following the guidelines included in the answer key, also found on the CD-ROM. Each unit test is available in two formats: as a PDF (portable document format) and as a Microsoft Word document. The Word documents are provided for those instructors who wish to customize the tests.

Online Unit-by-Unit Teaching Suggestions

The Unit-by-Unit Teaching Suggestions (downloadable at www.cambridge.org/grammarandbeyond) include unit-specific suggestions for expansion as well as the following suggestions.

- **Tech It Up:** Tips for using technology to practice the target grammar.
- **Beware:** Troubleshooting ideas for common problems with the target grammar.
- **Interact:** Ideas for games and other group activities that provide further practice.

Student's Book Ancillaries

The following resources enhance the learning experience.

Class Audio CD

The Class Audio CD provides all Student's Book listening material for in-class use.

Workbook

The Workbook provides additional practice of the grammar presented in the Student's Book. All exercises can be assigned for homework or completed in class.

Writing Skills Interactive

Writing Skills Interactive is an online interactive program that provides instruction in key skills crucial for academic writing (writing effective topic sentences, avoiding sentence fragments, distinguishing between fact and opinion, etc.). The units of *Writing Skills Interactive* correspond to and build on Student's Book units through shared vocabulary and themes.

Program Highlights

- Each unit includes an animated presentation that provides interactive, dynamic instruction in the writing skill.
- Academic and content vocabulary introduced in the corresponding Student's Book unit are recycled and practiced through the use of additional theme-based contexts.
- The presentation in each *Writing Skills Interactive* unit is followed by focused practice with immediate feedback.
- The program allows students to work at their own pace and review instructional presentations as needed. It is ideal for individual practice, although it can also be used successfully in the classroom or computer lab.

This guide provides a variety of strategies to use with recurring unit sections and exercise types in the *Grammar and Beyond* Student's Book. For expansion activities, technology-related activities, and ideas developed for individual units, refer to the Unit-by-Unit Teaching Suggestions, downloadable free of charge at www.cambridge.org/grammarandbeyond.

Student Self-Assessment

Refer to the Unit-by-Unit Teaching Suggestions (which can be downloaded at www.cambridge.org/grammarandbeyond) for the list of the objectives for each unit. Write them on the board and ask students to copy them. Then have students do a quick self-assessment on each objective by choosing from the three options:

> *Self-Assessment, Unit _____*
> *Objective _____*
>
> ☐ *1. I know a lot about this and can use it easily.*
> ☐ *2. I know something about this but need more practice.*
> ☐ *3. I don't know very much about this.*

Revisit the statements when you have completed the unit so that students can assess their progress.

Pre-unit Assessment Strategies

Prior Knowledge of Target Grammar

Before you begin the unit, you will probably want to do a quick assessment of students' prior knowledge of the grammar point. A grammar pre-assessment helps you determine whether students understand the meaning of the structure, whether they can describe and produce the form, and whether they are able to integrate it into their writing and spontaneous speech. Here are some ways to help you obtain this information quickly.

- To determine whether students understand the target language, write several sentences on the board using the structure. (*When the twins met, they discovered that they had studied the same subjects. They were very similar even though they had grown up apart.*) Ask questions (*Did they meet first or did they study first? Why is the sentence in the past perfect?*) to ensure that students grasp the meaning of the sentences.
- To determine whether students can describe and reproduce the form, ask them to identify, for example, the part of speech, verb forms, or auxiliaries of the target structure. (*What are the verbs in this sentence? What forms are they? How do you form the past perfect?*) Write several key words on the board. For example, write a

sentence with a relative clause if relative clauses are the target grammar structure. Then ask students to write sentences with the target structure(s). Walk around and spot-check their sentences to assess students' familiarity with the structure.

- If most of the students are able to write correct sentences, check their ability to use the grammar in a more extended activity by assigning a writing prompt. (*What happened in the news yesterday? What caused it to happen?*) Have them respond in writing with a four- or five-sentence paragraph. Remind them to use the target structure if they can. Collect their work so you can assess the class as a whole (and not just a few students). You can also use this information for pairing and grouping later. Note the grammar used in students' responses, but don't correct or begin teaching the structure explicitly at this point. Tell students that they will be learning the structure in the upcoming unit. You may want to keep the paragraphs and write some of the students' sentences on the board when you have completed the unit so they can identify their errors and see evidence of their progress.

If many of the students are able to produce the structure correctly in response to your question, you can move more quickly through the controlled practice in the unit and spend more time on the extended, open-ended writing and speaking activities. Tell students that although they may be familiar with the structure, it is your objective to help them put the grammar to use in their speaking and writing.

General Strategies for Unit Sections

Grammar in the Real World

This section introduces the target structure(s) in an authentic context, such as an article. A *Notice* activity draws students' attention to the form or function of the target structures in the text. The following strategies can be used with this section. See the Unit-by-Unit Teaching Suggestions at www.cambridge.org/grammarandbeyond for text-specific notes and vocabulary lists.

Pre-reading/Warm Up

- Direct students' attention to the picture. Ask them to describe it, or ask specific questions about it. (*What's happening? Who/Where do you think the person is?*) Ask students about their personal experiences or opinions related to the picture. (*Have you ever done this? How do you feel when this happens to you? What do you think about this?*)
- Ask students to read the title of the text and make one or two predictions about the content. Write students' predictions on the board. After they have read the text, compare their predictions to what they have read.

Pre-teaching the Vocabulary

Before students read, look through the text and make a list of words they may not know. Alternatively, use the word list, with Academic Word List (AWL) vocabulary labeled, found in the Unit-by-Unit Teaching Suggestions at www.cambridge.org/grammarandbeyond. Try one or both of these techniques:

- List the words on the board and ask students to discuss the meanings in small groups. Ask students for definitions. Make a note of words that students find difficult.
- List the words on one side of the board and their corresponding definitions on the other side (in a different order) and ask students to match them. Have students write down any words that are new. To save time in class, write the words and definitions on separate large cards in advance and post them where students can see them.

Glossed Vocabulary

Paying attention to text signals, like footnotes, is an important academic skill. Therefore, you may not want to include the glossed vocabulary among the words you pre-teach. Instead, draw students' attention to the footnote numbers and encourage them to watch for them while reading. Provide any clarification students need for the glossed words.

Comprehension Check

- To accommodate a variety of levels, have students complete the *Comprehension Check* individually. Write an additional comprehension question or a related question on the board for early finishers to answer.
- If you think the activity is challenging for some of your students, have them compare their answers with a partner before you review the answers as a class. This gives students a low-stress way of checking their work. Consider pairing students of different levels.

Notice

- The *Notice* activity guides students to find the target language in the text. Explain that scanning quickly for specific words is often an effective way to find the target language. (For example, suggest that they look for the word *had* in the unit on the past perfect.) To get them started, have students look at item 1 and tell you which word or words they should scan for.
- In some cases, you may want students to try to complete the activity before they read the text. Ask students to share their answers. Then have students scan the article to find the correct answers.
- Have students do the first part of the activity (finding the target language) individually. Then have them work in pairs to discuss the question or complete the final part of the activity.

Grammar Presentations

Each unit includes at least two of these sections, which provide presentations of the target grammar. They address both structure and usage, and offer examples that reflect the unit theme. The sections may also include a *Data from the Real World* box, providing real-world usage notes based on corpus research.

Overview Box

Read the information in the overview box that introduces each set of grammar charts. Explain that this box highlights a key feature of the grammar point. Ask students what the connection is between the introductory information and the example sentences.

Grammar Charts

Teach students the value of the charts as a reference tool. When they make mistakes, ask them to look at the relevant chart to self-correct. If possible, keep a copy of the relevant chart(s) visible in the classroom for easy reference. Following are some ways to present the charts in class.

Structure Charts

Some charts focus students' attention on forming the target language. Here are some possibilities for teaching structure charts.

- Have students start the lesson with books closed. Write one of the examples from the chart on the board. Ask questions to check students' understanding of the grammar. (*What's the verb in this sentence? What structure is it? How do you form it?*) Ask students to provide additional examples.
- Ask students if they can provide examples for the other structures covered in the chart (for example, if they can transform an affirmative sentence to a negative sentence or a question). If students are not able to do this, write the structure on the board and have students identify its components (for example, *auxiliary, subject, main verb*).
- Use the chart for structured question-and-answer practice by having students write three questions with the target structure. Then have them ask and answer their questions in pairs.
- Have students write additional examples.

Usage Charts

Some charts, like the one that follows, contain usage notes on the left and example sentences on the right, with the target language in boldface type. Here are some possibilities for teaching usage charts.

a. Use *since* with specific dates or times to show the start of an event that continues into the present moment.	*She **hasn't worked** here **since 2008**.* *He **has lived** here **since last year**.*
b. Use *for* to show the duration of time of an event that continues into the present moment.	*She **hasn't worked** here **for several years**.*
c. In negative sentences, the preposition *in* may replace *for*.	*She **hasn't seen** her **in several years**.*

- Discuss each usage note and read the example sentences. Ask students to identify texts or conversations where they encounter the target language. Elicit the target grammar by asking questions. To check present perfect forms, for example, you may ask *How long has the current president been in office? What has he done recently?*
- Write a variety of examples on the board for each usage note (or distribute the examples on paper to students). Ask students to work in pairs to match the usage notes from the chart with the new examples.
- Ask students to work in small groups to come up with an additional example for each note. You can add challenge by asking students to incorporate the unit theme and related vocabulary.

Data from the Real World

These boxes contain research-based usage information, informed by the world's largest corpus. Go over them with the students. Where appropriate, ask for additional examples and discuss students' own impressions or "real world" experiences with the target language.

For example, if the box says, "Some adverbs are more common in academic writing than in speaking," have students write two examples for the less formal and the more formal situations. (*The bank usually opens at 8:00* vs. *Banks typically provide multiple options for saving.*)

The Unit-by-Unit Teaching Suggestions, available at www.cambridge.org/grammarandbeyond, provide additional activities for practice of the information in these boxes.

Additional Presentation Strategies

Photos and Art

Use pictures from magazines or the Internet. Choose images that represent familiar events or topics that students will be able to talk about at some length. Give students a few minutes to talk about the picture. Then ask them to write a paragraph about the picture and to include several examples of the target structure. Have them share their writing in groups, checking for correct use of the structure.

Time Lines

Use time lines to talk about tenses. List events on the timeline and ask questions to elicit the target grammar. (*What can you tell me about this situation? How long had the twins been apart? How long had the scientists been studying the twins when they met?*)

Unit-by-Unit Teaching Suggestions

Refer to the Teaching Suggestions for each unit for help with potential trouble spots with the specific target grammar, exceptions to the rules, and unit-specific chart presentation activities. The Unit-by-Unit Teaching Suggestions can be downloaded free of charge at www.cambridge.org/grammarandbeyond.

Grammar Application

This section follows each Grammar Presentation and gives students practice with the target grammar in a variety of contexts. The exercises progress from more controlled to more open-ended practice, and incorporate the use of all four major skills (reading, writing, listening, speaking). Opportunities for personalization are also offered.

This section of the Student's Book practices the target grammar in a variety of theme-related contexts. The recurring exercise types are listed below with classroom strategies given for each. See the Unit-by-Unit Teaching Suggestions for specific writing, speaking, and other expansion activities, as well as suggestions for incorporating the use of technology.

Sentence Completion and Matching Activities

For these activities, have students work individually. To ensure that students are processing the information, and to expand on the activities, ask them to do one or more of the following:

- Explain the choice they made using information from the usage chart.
- Check and discuss their answers with a partner.
- Write another example on the board for their classmates to complete.

Listening Activities

Follow these steps with the listening activities.

1. Direct students to read the activity before they listen in order to prepare them for what they will hear. To make the activity more challenging, have them guess the answers before listening.

2. Play the audio once all the way through at normal speed and without pausing. Be sure to tell students that you will play it again. Then play it again, pausing after each item if students need time to finish writing. Play it a third time, again at normal speed.

3. When you reach the end of the exercise, direct students to read through it again. You may want students to compare their answers with a partner's so that they can check for potential errors.

4. Go over the answers by having students write them on the board (one student can write four or five answers), or project the exercise with an overhead or LCD projector, and complete it together.

Writing Activities

In these activities, students write sentences about their own ideas. Be sure that they receive feedback on their work. Try one or more of these techniques:

■ Have students share their sentences in small groups and then compile a group version of the activity, choosing at least one sentence from each member. Then have the groups exchange papers and discuss any errors in form or usage. Monitor their discussions and note mistakes to discuss with the entire class.

■ Have students put sentences on the board. While they are writing, walk around and spot-check the work of other students.

Avoid Common Mistakes

This section presents a few of the most common learner errors associated with the target grammar, based on the world's largest error-coded learner corpus. It develops students' awareness of common mistakes and gives them an opportunity to practice identifying and correcting these errors in an editing exercise.

The information in this section is based on an extensive database of authentic student writing, so you can be sure that the errors indicated are truly high-frequency. This prepares students for the self-editing stage in the Grammar for Writing section, and reminds them of the importance of self-editing in all their writing. If you see these mistakes during unit activities (or even after you've moved on to later units) refer students to the box in this section, rather than correcting them yourself. The Unit-by-Unit Teaching Suggestions often provide further examples of common mistakes.

Editing Task

Have students work individually to complete the task and then compare answers with a partner. Do one of the following to correct the text.

■ Ask two or more students to read the corrected version aloud. Be sure to call on different students each time, so all feel accountable.

■ Use an LCD or overhead projector to have students work together to correct the text.

■ Let students know if they miss a mistake, and tell them the category it falls under in the *Avoid Common Mistakes* box. Ask them to search the text again.

Grammar for Writing

This section provides an assignment designed to support students as they incorporate the grammar into their own writing.

The Grammar for Writing box contains a quick review of the unit grammar as it relates to the writing assignment. Use the following strategies to teach each stage of this section.

Pre-writing Task

Follow these steps to complete the Exercise:

1. Go over the information in the box and tell students they will be focusing on these points for both the Pre-writing Task and the Writing Task.

2. Have students complete the Pre-writing Task individually and ask them to compare their answers with a partner.

3. Ask students for the answers. If possible, type the answers using a computer connected to an LCD projector, or write the answers on a copy of the page projected with an overhead projector.

Writing Task

Refer to the Unit-by-Unit Teaching Suggestions, available for download free of charge at www.cambridge.org/grammarandbeyond, for unit-specific ideas and alternative writing tasks. Follow these steps for the activities in the Student's Book:

1. Help students come up with ideas in one of the following ways.

   ■ Ask questions to facilitate a whole-class brainstorming session. (What does the writer of the paragraph in the Pre-writing Task say about this topic? What are some things you might say about it?)

   ■ Seat students in groups, and have each group brainstorm. Then have the groups share their ideas with the class.

2. Draw students' attention to the structure of the paragraph in the Pre-writing Task, such as topic and concluding sentences, supporting details, or word choice. Ask them to use the same features in their writing.

3. Assign the writing task as homework, or give students time to finish it in class. If you are doing the activity in class, set a time limit to help students stay on task.

Self- and Peer Editing

The following are strategies for encouraging both self- and peer editing.

- Have students read the questions in the Self-Edit section of the Writing Task, and ask them to read through their writing and make changes as necessary.
- Have students exchange papers with a partner. Ask the partners to underline examples of the target language and check it against the *Avoid Common Mistakes* box. Have them circle any errors. Tell the partners to discuss any mistakes they found before they return the papers for revision.
- Have students peer-edit in groups of three, focusing on one paper at a time.
- Collect the students' writing and note the errors the students circle (or circle any mistakes with the target language that you see). Use these as examples in a follow-up lesson by writing the circled sentences on the board or typing them up and projecting them for class correction.

Grouping Strategies

It is difficult to overestimate the value of using a variety of grouping strategies in the classroom. In addition to making the class more dynamic, it helps you address different learning styles. Time for individual work is important because it allows students to process material in their own ways, but there are also many advantages to pair and group work.

Setting Up Groups

- **To create random groups**, pass out "four of a kind" items, such as different colored slips of paper or playing cards. Then ask students to stand, and guide them to different areas of the room: *Everyone with a blue paper come over here.* Alternatively, you can have students count off in threes or fours. Once they have counted, ask for a show of hands. (*All Number 1s, raise your hand.*) Then have all students with the same number sit together.
  Advantage: Helps build classroom community, challenges students to "get out of their shells," and increases the energy level of the class.
- **To create mixed-level groups,** use items that represent two or more levels. For example, pass out blue cards to higher-level students (or students who have performed best on an assessment) and white cards to lower-level students. Tell students to form groups consisting of, for example, two blue cards and two white cards.
  Advantage: Allows for peer tutoring, gives lower-level students exposure to higher-level English, helps lower-level students feel like an integral part of the class.
- **To create same-level groups,** use the same strategy as for mixed-level groups (items to represent levels). Tell students to form groups of all white cards or all blue cards.

Advantage: Allows you to tailor the activity to the level of the group (by simplifying it for the lower-level group or making it more challenging/open-ended for the higher-level group).

Pair Work

- For pair work that involves collaborative work, you may want to pair students of similar levels so that one isn't doing all of the work. Or pair students of different levels and give each partner a distinct role. (*Partner A says the question, and Partner B writes it down.*)
- For pair work that encourage repetition, such as interviews and surveys, conduct a "walk-around." Have students walk around the room and ask questions to multiple classmates.

Strategies for Multilevel Classrooms

Every class has students at different levels, whether the class is designated "multilevel" or not. Following are some ways to help lower- and higher-level students within multilevel contexts. It is important to use a variety of strategies to address different student needs. Too much separation of lower-level students may make them feel as though they don't belong in the class, and too much peer tutoring may be frustrating for higher-level students.

Lower-level Students

Use one or more of these techniques for working with lower-level students:

- Adapt activities for lower-level students so that they can focus on one task. For example, provide sentence frames for them to use while other students are writing open responses.
- Seat students in mixed-level groups and assign an easier role for lower-level students (for example, as the reporter who reads the group's answers to the class).

Higher-Level Students

- Provide more open-ended tasks for these students after they have completed the exercises in the book (for example, write additional items for an exercise and put them on the board for other students to complete, write additional interview questions).
- Adjust tasks to a more formal register for these students. For example, instead of asking them to "describe the person's appearance," tell them to describe the person's appearance as if they were describing a suspect in a court of law.
- Group higher-level students and give them a special project to complete while you work with lower-level students (e.g., write a story using four words from the Academic Word List and at least two examples of the target grammar).

Class Audio Script

Unit 1

Exercise 3.3: More Stative or Action Meaning?
A (p. 11 / track 2)

Reporter When you meet someone for the first time, how does the person's appearance affect your judgment? Today, we are asking people to describe how they make judgments about others.

Marta I know I use unfair stereotypes when I meet someone new. To me, older people always seem like they need help. When I meet an older person, I'm always thinking about my grandparents. I speak slowly and clearly, in case the person can't hear. I know it's wrong to think all older people are like that, but I can't help it.

Marc I feel that I am always very fair when I meet a new person. I know people's appearances don't always say who they really are. For example, if I meet a person who looks sloppy, I don't think that he or she is a lazy person.

Bin For me, it depends on the situation. When I am interviewing people at work, I take their appearance very seriously. For example, I always notice how a person dresses for an interview. If a person's appearance seems sloppy or careless in an interview, I think he or she will be a sloppy and careless worker.

Unit 2

Exercise 4.2: Used To, Would, or Simple Past?
A and B (p. 26 / track 3)

Zach How has TV advertising changed over the years?

Dave In the past, we used to create commercials with very direct messages. Commercials used to tell the consumer exactly what to do. We never used to be vague about the message at all. In addition, commercials didn't use to try to entertain the viewer.

Zach So, how would you create an advertising message in the old days?

Dave A commercial for our product would say: "Drink Fruity Juice." We would show the product several times in a commercial. We didn't use to hide the product.

Zach What changed?

Dave We saw some research a few years ago. It showed that people no longer pay attention to commercials like those. As a result, we decided to change our style. Now we are producing "mystery ads." Mystery ads don't show the product until the very end of the commercial. They entertain the viewer because the viewer has to figure out what the product is.

Unit 3

Exercise 4.2: Simple Past, Present Perfect, and Present Perfect Progressive
C (p. 41 / track 4)

Zaha Hadid is an architect. She has designed many famous buildings around the world, including the Rosenthal Center for Contemporary Art in Cincinnati. Hadid was born in Iraq, and she studied architecture in London in the late 1970s. Since the 1980s, she has been working at a design company, and she has been teaching architecture at several universities.

Richard Branson is one of the world's most successful businesspeople. He was born in England. He had a hard time in school because he had a learning disability. Reading was difficult for him. As a result, he left school at age 16. After that, he started his first business. Later, he opened a record shop called Virgin Records. Since then, he has started new businesses in many different industries, including transportation, entertainment, and communications.

Unit 4

Exercise 2.3: More Past Perfect and Simple Past
A and B (pp. 50–51 / track 5)

Claudia Today, I'm interviewing Alex and Andrew Underhill. They appear in the *Spy Twins* movie series based on the books of the same name. How did you get the part in the first *Spy Twins* movie?

Alex A friend had seen the advertisement in the newspaper and later told us about it. We hadn't done any acting before then, but we decided to try out anyway.

Claudia How many twins were at the audition?

Andrew When we got there, we saw that about five other sets of twins had shown up for the audition.

Alex We also noticed that all the twins were wearing matching outfits. Until that audition, we had never worn the same clothes in our whole lives. We decided to run out to the nearest shopping mall to buy some matching clothes. The audition had just started when we returned.

Claudia Had you read the *Spy Twins* novels before your audition?

Andrew   Yes. The third book had come out when we went to the first audition.

Claudia   What's it like being twins? Are you two close? Do you do the same things?

Alex   Yes, in lots of ways.

Andrew   We definitely think the same way.

Alex   Right! Once, we took the same test in school. Of course, we were in the same grade, but we had different teachers. We had exactly the same answers correct, even though we hadn't been in the same classroom!

Claudia   Wow! I guess you're a lot alike in many ways! Well, thanks, Alex and Andrew. It's been great talking with you.

Unit 5

Exercise 3.2: More *Will* or *Be Going To*?

A (p. 69 / track 6)

Ms. Ng   Will everyone please be quiet? The noise is going to make it hard to hear our speaker. And will someone please open the windows? The air conditioner isn't working well.

Alex   I'll do it.

Ms. Ng   Thanks. And will you all please turn off your cell phones? I promise I won't ask you to do anything else except enjoy today's presentation. OK, today, we're going to hear from an expert on education, Dr. Paul Bell. I'm sure you will all find him very interesting.

Dr. Bell   Thank you. Well, it's clear that the world of the college student is going to be very different in a matter of a few years. For example, we already know that colleges will offer more courses online. This will save money for schools and for students. Students will save money on transportation costs because they can learn anywhere. Online learning also means that schools and individuals will use fewer resources such as paper and fuel. But what will the consequences of online education be?

Unit 6

Exercise 3.3: Time Clauses with Future Perfect and Future Perfect Progressive

A and B (p. 86 / track 7)

1. Will the company have found a temporary site for the workers by the time it approves the building plans?
2. Will the company have moved into the temporary site before construction starts?
3. Will the construction firm have finished all the construction work by the time it installs the solar heating system?
4. Once the construction ends, will the company have worked at the temporary site for longer than a year?

5. By the time the company moves back into the building, will the designer have installed the new workstations?
6. Will OSHA have visited by the time the company sends the report on building improvements to the finance department?
7. Will the company have worked in the remodeled building for one year by the time the new law starts?
8. By the time OSHA visits the offices, will the employees have been at the remodeled building for two years?

Unit 7

Exercise 3.4: More Present and Future Necessity and Obligation

A and B (p. 99 / track 8)

1. Participants have to attend two sessions.
2. Sessions are supposed to be two hours.
3. Participants must be younger than 18 years of age.
4. Each participant has to have good vision.
5. Each participant must have normal hearing.
6. Participants must speak Mandarin.
7. Participants do not have to be students at the university.
8. Participants are required to e-mail the researcher by July 31st.

Unit 8

Exercise 3.2: More Future Probability

A and B (pp. 112–113 / track 9)

Conversation 1

Anne   Someone broke into the Lees' apartment, and now they're moving.

Martín   That's awful. Where are they going to go?

Anne   I'm not sure. They'll probably move to the suburbs.

Martín   But Joe Lee has a good job here in the city. They may not be able to move very far away.

Anne   I know. And the children are in school in the city. They might not want to change schools.

Martín   Well, I wish them luck.

Conversation 2

Truong   I spoke with Andrew Martinez yesterday. Guess what? He may buy a home security system.

Ben   I know. We went to a home security show last week. He liked the system with the cameras that send images to your phone. That might be the system he's going to buy.

Truong   I could learn a lot from Andrew when he puts in his system.

Conversation 3

Radio Reporter   The airport commissioner announced today that Bay City Airport will start using cameras with sensors that will detect heart rate and body temperature. They should be ready by next year.

Josh	I read about the cameras online as well. In fact, I heard that they could start using the cameras by the end of this year.
Katie	It'll be interesting to see what happens.

Unit 9

Exercise 4.3: More Order of Adjectives
A and B (p. 132 / track 10)

Last week, we ate at Le Bambou, an elegant new Vietnamese restaurant in town. We ordered several delicious small dishes. We highly recommend the fresh, delicious spring rolls. They were a spicy vegetarian appetizer, and they were perfect for the lovely, warm evening. The main course was a large, traditional chicken dish served with fresh, crisp vegetables.

We were especially impressed with Le Bambou's atmosphere. It has a beautiful, cozy dining room. The tables were covered with cotton and silk tablecloths, and they were all lit by tall white candles in silver and gold holders. The walls were painted a lovely shade of blue, and the color gave the restaurant a sense of calm. The serving dishes looked like rare, expensive antiques. There were beautiful green and gold dragons on the plates.

All in all, Le Bambou was a delicious and memorable experience.

Unit 10

Exercise 2.2: A/An, The, or No Article?
A (p. 140 / track 11)

Color Harmony

Some colors go together while some colors don't. Why? Is there a way to understand why some colors work better together than others? As many artists and designers know, color harmony is based on color theory.

Let's think about the ways color harmony works in a room. One main rule of color harmony is that one color must be stronger than the other colors in the room. In other words, one color must be more intense than the others or cover a larger area than the others.

Another rule of color harmony is that you should not put two very intense colors next to each other. For example, you should not have a bright red sofa on top of a bright green rug. The human eye cannot focus on both colors at the same time, and the colors may seem to vibrate.

A third rule of color harmony is that the colors in a room should be related to each other in some way. You can determine colors' relationships to each other by looking at a color wheel. Colors that are next to each other on the color wheel, such as red and red-orange, will usually look good together. You can also put complementary colors together. These are colors that are on opposite sides of the color wheel, such as yellow and purple. Color triads go

well together, too. These are three colors that are the same distance from each other on the color wheel. For example, the primary colors, red, blue, and yellow, form a color triad. The secondary colors, green, purple, and orange, also form a color triad.

Exercise 3.3: Using Quantifiers with *Of*
(p. 145 / track 12)

Mark	Recently, our university hired some interior designers and color experts to redesign the interior of the library at Bay City University. I asked a group of students at the college what they thought about this. Here's what they said:
Josh	Some of my friends don't like it. They think the colors are too bright. Some people don't like to study at the library because the bright colors make them uncomfortable.
Amy	All of my friends love the new colors, but we know that some people don't like the color choices. You can never please all of the people when you make a change, though.
Lynn	A few of the people I know think it's great! They like being surrounded by a lot of bright colors. I think a few students would probably prefer to have softer colors in the library, though.
Paolo	None of my friends study in the library anymore. All of them study in the dorms because they don't like the colors in the library. But I like the new design. There were no students studying on the first floor of the library this morning, so I had the whole place to myself.

Unit 11

Exercise 4.2: More Indefinite Pronouns
B (p. 160 / track 13)

Jane	You get more vacation time than the average American, don't you? I wonder about other countries. Do you know anything about vacation time in different places around the world?
Adam	I do, but it tends to vary depending on what source you look at. I think that no one has more paid time off than people in the European Union. On average, they get 25 to 30 paid vacation days per year, with a minimum of 20!
Jane	Wow. That's a lot more than in Mexico, where they get, on average, 6 to 14 days of vacation. What's the average in the United States?
Adam	Nobody gets less than people in the United States because there is actually no minimum here for paid days off. We usually get about 7 to 14 paid days off per year. And a lot of people don't even take all their vacation time.
Jane	Well, you can't go anywhere really far in only 7 to 14 days, can you? What about Asia? Do you know anything about vacation time in Asia?

Adam   It's not much. I think that they get about 5 days in the Philippines, and only 6 in Thailand. South Koreans get about 10 paid vacation days.

Jane   Wow. That's not much. What about Japan?

Adam   The Japanese get about 11 days of vacation. In Canada, it's generally around at least 10, but it varies among provinces.

Jane   Wow! So, Americans' vacation habits are similar to those of people in Canada, Japan, and South Korea.

Adam   I think you're right. It would be great to have more time off than we do.

Unit 12

Exercise 3.3: Gerunds with Common Fixed Expressions

B (p. 172 / track 14)

Conversation 1

A   I've heard some crazy excuses for not handing in papers.

B   I don't think there's any good reason for not doing your work once you're in college.

Conversation 2

A   You spend a lot of time studying. Does it help?

B   Yes, I would have trouble keeping up with my classes if I didn't spend a lot of time studying.

Conversation 3

A   A lot of people waste time partying in college. What do you plan on doing after you leave this school?

B   I have an interest in getting a bachelor's degree, so I plan on transferring to a four-year institution.

Conversation 4

A   What type of student is the Joe Olinsky Foundation in favor of giving grants to?

B   We have money from a government fund that we use for students who would otherwise have difficulty affording a two-year college.

Unit 13

Exercise 3.2: Infinitive or Gerund?

A and B (p. 185 / track 15)

Jocelyn   So, Bo, I hear you have some unpleasant news.

Bo   Yes . . . well, I'll try starting at the beginning.

Jocelyn   Please do.

Bo   OK. I regret to say that our product placement in *Jake's Life* isn't working. We tried doing things differently this time, but it just didn't work.

Jocelyn   That's OK. We hired you to find these things out. I certainly don't regret hiring you. So, please tell us the results.

Bo   Well, here's what happened. The group watched all six episodes of *Jake's Life*. We told them to push

a button each time they saw Jake drinking a soda. Some remember seeing Jake order a soda, but only 15 percent remembered the name of the soda.

Jocelyn   That's certainly not good.

Bo   Here are some of their comments:

    Participant 1: "This show is boring. I stopped watching after the third episode."

    Participant 2: "I remember seeing the café scene, but it made me hungry. I paused the show and stopped to get a snack. I forgot to turn the show back on after I got something to eat. So I didn't see all of the show."

    Participant 3: "I remember the café scene, but I don't remember seeing Jake drink anything."

Jocelyn   Excuse me, Bo. Did all of them follow the directions? Did anyone forget to push the button when Jake drank soda?

Bo   No. Nobody did. Here's Participant 4: "I remembered to push the button each time I saw Jake drinking a soda, but I don't remember the name of the drink."

    Participant 5 –

Jocelyn   Stop reading, Bo! I get the picture!

Unit 14

Exercise 3.5: Pronunciation Focus: Intonation and Meaning in Tag Questions

(p. 198 / track 16)

Use rising intonation in the tag when you are not certain your statement is true.	*"Moving wasn't difficult, **was it**?"* ↗ *"Yes, it was!"* *"There won't be a quiz tomorrow,* ↘↗ ***will there**?"* *"No, there won't."*
Use falling intonation when you expect the listener to agree with you.	*"His research is really boring, **isn't it**?"* ↘ *"Yes, it is."* *"You didn't go to class, **did you**?"* ↘ *"No, I didn't."*

A (p. 198 / track 17)

Moving wasn't difficult, was it? ↗

There won't be a quiz tomorrow, will there? ↗

His research is really boring, isn't it? ↘

You didn't go to class, did you? ↘

B (p. 198 / track 18)

Conversation 1

Mother   You're not still thinking about going to college in Pennsylvania, are you? ↘↗

Son   Yes, Mom. We've discussed this many times.

Mother   But that college doesn't offer the major you want, does it? ↘↗

Son	No, but I'm not certain that's what I want to major in.	*Paula*	I'm impressed! I wonder why she invented it.

Conversation 2

Woman   Your son is thinking of going to college far from home, isn't he?

Mother   Yes. He's thinking of going to Duquesne University.

Woman   Duquesne University is in Pittsburgh, isn't it?

Mother   That's right.

Conversation 3

Woman   You're excited about moving to Pennsylvania for college, aren't you?

Son   Yes, I am.

Woman   You're not worried about moving so far from home, are you?

Son   A little bit.

Conversation 4

Woman   Your son is worried about moving so far from home, isn't he?

Father   Yes, I'm afraid he is.

Woman   But you and your wife feel OK about him moving so far away, don't you?

Father   I feel OK about it, but my wife doesn't.

Unit 15

Exercise 3.2: *That* Clauses in Sentences with Past Verbs in the Main Clause

(p. 209 / track 19)

    In the nineteenth century, many people believed that Americans had the right to expand across the continent. John Quincy Adams, the sixth president of the United States, thought that one large country would be good for all Americans. However, some people knew that the westward expansion would have some negative consequences. For example, some people were aware that westward expansion was having a negative impact on Native American culture. In fact, some Americans at the time felt that the U.S. government was taking Native American land unfairly. They also pointed out that westward expansion was leading to many wars, such as the Mexican-American War of 1836. Most people did not realize that Americans were destroying native plants and wildlife as well.

Unit 16

Exercise 2.1: Noun Clauses with *Wh-* Words

A (pp. 218–219 / track 20)

Peter   OK, let's start with Randi Altschul.

Larry   I don't know who Randi Altschul is.

Paula   Neither do I. I don't know what she invented.

Peter   I know who she is. She invented the disposable cell phone.

Paula   I'm impressed! I wonder why she invented it.

Larry   I don't know.

Peter   Got it! It says here her cell phone wasn't working well, and she felt like throwing it away.

Larry   Let's find out when she invented it.

Peter   It says here she got a patent for it in 1999.

Larry   I just found out where she was living at the time. It was Florida.

Paula   I wonder what the cell phone looked like.

Peter   It says here that it was only 2 inches by 3 inches – kind of like a credit card.

Larry   I wonder what it was made of.

Peter   It was made of recycled paper.

Unit 17

Exercise 5.2: More Reporting Verbs

A and B (pp. 239–240 / track 21)

David   What happened in class today?

Mira   We had a guest speaker. He told us about the importance of motivation in the language classroom. He reminded us there are two kinds of motivation: intrinsic and extrinsic.

David   Right. Last week, the professor suggested that there were two different types, and she gave examples.

Mira   Yes. So, anyway, the speaker stated that he had done a study of students in Japan and students in the United States. He mentioned that both groups had native-speaking English teachers. He explained that the purpose of the study was to see whether the teachers' remarks had a negative effect on the motivation of the Japanese students.

David   What did he find out?

Mira   He reported that the study found four ways in which the teachers' behavior had a negative effect on Japanese students' motivation.

David   Did he give any examples?

Mira   He claimed that classroom discussion is one area where there are key differences. He informed us that in the Japanese classroom, students generally listen more and talk less.

David   And as we know from our reading, Porter and Samovar showed that in the U.S. classroom, some students speak up spontaneously, and that a lot of teachers encourage discussion.

Mira   Right. So, he explained that when a teacher criticizes a Japanese group for not participating, it has a bad effect on motivation.

Unit 18

Exercise 3.2: Indirect Requests and Advice

(p. 250 / track 22)

Therapist   In order to help you improve your relationship, you first need to know what a good relationship is. Let's get started. Please take a pad of paper and a pencil. Ready? Please describe your ideal marriage.

Husband May I take a different pencil, please?
Therapist Of course.
Wife May I use my own pen?
Therapist Certainly. Now, you should write for 15 minutes without stopping. You should not look at each other's writing during the activity. You should not talk to each other, either. You should be prepared to read your descriptions to each other.
Husband May I have a little more time to write?
Therapist No, the activity works best if you only write for 15 minutes.

Unit 19

Exercise 4.1: Describing Processes and Results
A and B (pp. 263–264 / track 23)

A recent study showed that grammar instruction improves ESL students' essays. One hundred students were put into two groups at the beginning of a semester. At the beginning of the semester, students in each group were given an essay-writing assignment. Then, throughout the semester, group 1 was taught essay-writing techniques only. Students in group 2, however, were taught both essay-writing techniques and grammar. At the end of the semester, both groups wrote a final essay. The first and final essays were read by a group of judges. The judges compared the first essays with the final essays. They put essays that were easier to read and understand into a special folder. All of the final essays from both group 1 and group 2 were put into the folder. None of the first essays from either group were added to the folder. This indicates that all students learned something during the semester.

Then all the final essays were analyzed again. The judges rated all of the final essays from both groups. The essays were rated from 1 to 5, with 5 being the best. Most of the final essays produced by group 2 received ratings of 4 or 5. Most of the final essays produced by group 1 were given ratings of 2 or 3. The results seem to indicate that ESL students' writing improves when grammar and writing instruction are included in the same course.

Unit 20

Exercise 4.2: More Passive Gerunds and Infinitives
A (pp. 277–278 / track 24)

Reporter Hello to everyone. Today I'll be asking people their thoughts on food labeling. First, let's talk to Andrew. Andrew, do you read food labels?
Andrew I refuse to be forced to do so much work when I go shopping! I just want to be sold decent, healthy food. No, I don't read them.

Reporter I can understand that. Al and Mei?
Al We expect to be told the truth by food companies, but we know labels aren't always accurate.
Mei You have to inform yourself. All consumers have to start being better informed, so we always read them.
Reporter OK. And you, Roxana, do you read food labels?
Roxana Yes, because I'm a pretty informed consumer. I'm not too concerned about being fooled by food companies, but I'm not interested in being poisoned, either!
Reporter Thank you, Roxana. And finally, Jessica. What do you think?
Jessica It's sometimes easy to be fooled by product labeling, so I don't read them much because they don't matter. Take the word *natural*, for example. You expect it to be used for food that has few or no artificial ingredients. However, the word *natural* can be used for genetically modified food products.
Reporter Thanks to you all. It appears that consumers are tired of being confused by food companies.

Unit 21

Exercise 2.1: Subject Relative Pronouns
B (p. 285 / track 25)

Silvia is a student at Bay City University (BCU) who works out at the campus gym every day. Today, she is exercising on a bike which connects to a power grid. Silvia is possibly producing the energy which keeps the gym lights on or which powers a professor's laptop in another part of the campus. BCU and Bay City Tech are just two educational institutions which use human energy as power.

We interviewed Mark Sandoval, a BCU employee who runs campus operations. He said, "This is not a program which saves the university money. It's more of an experiment which illustrates to the students how they affect their environment." GreenGo is a Bay City human energy company which provides BCU with the exercise equipment. Rita Crane, a GreenGo spokesperson, said, "We enjoy working with students and faculty who take their impact on the environment very seriously."

Unit 22

Exercise 4.1: Prepositions and Object Relative Clauses
A and B (pp. 303–304 / track 26)

I arrived at the crime scene at 11:00 a.m. The crime had taken place in a restaurant. The room that the crime occurred in was the kitchen. The back door was open. The back wall was covered in graffiti. I found a spray can under a table. The spray can, which I found fingerprints on, matched the color of the graffiti. I asked the kitchen staff to talk to me as a group. The group, from which the chef was the only one missing, was very nervous. I learned that the chef had a lot of enemies. I spoke to a cleaning person who the chef had argued with last week. I also interviewed several waitresses that the chef had gone out with. One waitress showed me the chef's locker, which I found more spray cans in.

Unit 23

Exercise 2.2: More Object Relative Clauses with *Where* and *When*
A, B, and C (pp. 311–312 / track 27)

Interviewer Some people think that members of the Millennial generation only think about themselves, but there are a lot of young people who are making a difference. They are helping others and trying to make the world a better place. One of these young people is Sean Green. Sean is a medical student in Florida. He went to Haiti at a time in which they needed him the most. Sean, tell us your story.

Sean Sure, I'd be happy to. I went to Haiti at a time when many people were suffering – right after the 2010 earthquake.

Interviewer Why did you go?

Sean Haiti is a place where there aren't enough doctors. I'm in medical school now. So it seemed like a good opportunity for me to get experience and to help people as well.

Interviewer What did you do there?

Sean I worked in small towns in which the earthquake destroyed the homes of many people. I lived in a town where a lot of people were hurt and helped give basic medical care. It was the season during which there is a lot of rain. There was mud everywhere. It was a challenge to keep things clean.

Interviewer Tell us a little about the people you worked with.

Sean The people in the town in which I worked gave us a lot of help. They were very friendly and welcoming. It was an amazing experience.

Interviewer Thank you for your time, Sean.

Unit 24

Exercise 4.3: Real Conditionals with Modals, Modal-like Expressions, and Imperatives
A and B (p. 332 / track 28)

Interviewer Today, with the election coming up, we're talking about how to become an informed

voter. With me is Alicia Wong from the League of Women Voters.

Well, Ms. Wong, I think we all agree on one thing: if you don't like the way things are, you should change them. And the best part is that you *can* change things if you aren't happy. That's what voting is all about. But a lot of us aren't sure how to make the best choices. What advice do you have for first-time voters, or for people who just want to become better informed?

Alicia Wong Whenever an election is coming up, you must first make sure you're registered. If you aren't registered to vote, register early so you don't miss the deadline. If you aren't registered by a certain date, you may miss out on the opportunity to vote.

Now, here are some more suggestions. If you want to be an informed voter, visit the local campaign headquarters for the candidates of both parties. It's also a good idea to attend campaign rallies for both parties. If you want to make the right choice, you must also visit the websites of all the candidates. Do not rely on campaign ads for information about the candidates or the issues if you want to be an informed voter. Don't pay attention to what media sources say about a candidate, either, if you want the truth.

Finally, don't let other people's opinions influence your vote if you want to make good choices. If you want more information, please visit the League of Women Voters' website.

Interviewer Thank you, Ms. Wong. I think you've given us some very useful tips.

Unit 25

Exercise 3.2: Past Unreal Conditionals: Regret
B and C (p. 344 / track 29)

I was camping with a few friends in the forest on Mount St. Helens the day the volcano erupted. We didn't hear a sound; we just saw a great ash cloud in the sky. I think we only survived because the force of the explosion threw us into a hole. That way, the falling, burning trees didn't hit us. We walked several miles through the forest trying to get off the side of the mountain. The trees were still on fire. It's hard to imagine that anyone else who was on the mountain that day survived. Thankfully, my wife had decided not to come with us, so she wasn't affected.

No one knew how bad the damage would be because Mount St. Helens didn't erupt like a normal volcano. Experts had been expecting some sort of eruption, but not one that blew out the *side* of the mountain. This caused a great deal of damage. It caused an enormous landslide and killed 57 people, who lived and worked on the mountain.

Ten years later, my friends and I came back to the campsite. We were able to find exactly where we camped because part of our tent was still there. It was tough to go back. We were all so afraid for our lives.

Even though they couldn't predict the eruption, scientists did learn from the eruption. One thing scientists learned was how quickly nature can come back after a disaster like this. Plant and animal life returned very quickly after the eruption. It's nice to see that life here has gone on.

Unit 26

Exercise 4.2: Reducing Verb Forms
B and C (pp. 362–363 / track 30)

Interviewer	I'm speaking with Chef Hiro Noguchi, owner of East Wind Café. Chef Noguchi, I understand that Asian fusion is new in some European markets. What menu items are becoming popular?
Chef	Raw fish is getting more popular, and so is seaweed salad.
Interviewer	What kinds of raw fish do people order?
Chef	Mainly tuna. Tuna has been selling well, but eel hasn't. Jellyfish didn't sell well last month, and sea urchin didn't, either.
Interviewer	There must be many Asian dishes that seem familiar, though.
Chef	Yes, noodles, of course. Spicy noodles have sold well, and so have cold noodles.
Interviewer	You have a lot of Japanese and Chinese items on the menu. What other Asian dishes do you serve?
Chef	Thai, for one. But this restaurant can't get customers interested in Thai dishes, and our other restaurants can't, either.
Interviewer	What will you do?
Chef	We'll probably stop offering Thai dishes, and the other branches will, too.
Interviewer	What about Westernized Asian dishes such as chop suey?
Chef	We won't serve that, and most other Asian restaurants won't, either.
Interviewer	Well, everything looks quite authentic. What about desserts?
Chef	Here, we've adapted a little to local tastes. We have green tea ice cream and banana cake. The ice cream has been selling well, and the cake has, too.
Interviewer	That sounds delicious. Thanks, Chef Noguchi.

Unit 27

Exercise 2.2: More Adverb Clauses
B (p. 370 / track 31)

Jane	So, Claire, how did you know you were a shopping addict?
Claire	When I saw a show on TV, I realized I was an addict.
Jane	I understand that you're getting help.
Claire	Yes. Because my insurance pays for it, I was able to sign up for therapy.
Jane	Is your therapy helping?
Claire	Definitely. Although I've only been in therapy a short time, I'm feeling better already.
Jane	How are things different now?
Claire	Since I only buy what I really need, I'm spending much less money.
Jane	Describe a recent shopping trip.
Claire	Even though I was at the mall yesterday, I only went to one store. Since I had a list, I only bought things I truly needed.
Jane	Good for you! Thank you for sharing your story with us.

Unit 28

Exercise 3.1: Transition Words to Show Sequence
B and C (pp. 384–385 / track 32)

Every game designer has his or her own way of designing a video game. There are certain steps, though, that everyone follows. I've had 10 years of game designing experience, and here are the steps I follow.

First, I decide on an overall concept for a game, that is, the theme or the environment in which it takes place. By environment, I mean: Is it a sports game like *Football Fantasy II*? Is it space game like *Alien World War*? Or is it a lifestyle game like *Meet the Family*? Second, I figure out the goal of the game and the rules. This is easy once you've chosen the theme. Next, I do research on the theme. If it's a sports game, for instance, I have to make sure I know all the details of the sport just like a professional, because a lot of times, real athletes play these games, too. Then I use software to make a prototype of the game. A prototype is a working model of the game. It's kind of like the first draft of a piece of writing. It includes all the aspects of the game, but sometimes the art is unfinished. The idea is to see if the game itself works. In this phase, I test the game. I get other people to test it, too. I see if I've missed anything important. After that, I go back to the computer and make any necessary changes.

The game is basically done at this point, so finally, I work with the marketing people. I help them design the box for the game and write the marketing materials. That's it. The game is now ready for the stores, and I hope it sells a lot of copies!

Answer Key

1 Simple Present and Present Progressive
First Impressions

1 Grammar in the Real World

A page 2

Answers will vary.

B Comprehension Check page 3

Possible answers:
1. It takes less than 30 seconds.
2. It is helping to reveal our thinking processes, both conscious and subconscious.
3. Both young and old people tend to associate the word *good* with pictures of young people.

C Notice page 3

1. forms; general fact or habit
2. help; general fact or habit
3. are researching; temporary action
4. is investigating; temporary action
simple present: general facts or habits
present progressive: temporary actions

2 Simple Present vs. Present Progressive

Exercise 2.1 Simple Present page 5

2. helps	7. have
3. teaches	8. videotapes
4. meets	9. have
5. gives	10. starts
6. shows	

Exercise 2.2 Simple Present or Present Progressive? page 6

2. do Josh and Rachel work; Josh and Rachel / They work three times a week.
3. does Josh start his job; He/Josh starts his job at 9 in the morning.
4. Is Rachel talking; Yes, she/Rachel is talking to a student right now.
5. students are waiting; Three students are waiting in his/Josh's line.
6. Who is making; Rachel is making a better first impression on the students who need help.
7. does Rachel finish; She/Rachel finishes work at 1 in the afternoon.
8. Who is not helping; Josh is not helping students at the moment.

Exercise 2.3 More Simple Present or Present Progressive?

A page 7

2. takes	8. spends
3. begin	9. asks
4. continue	10. ends
5. are interviewing	11. expects
6. are meeting	12. are; looking
7. take	

B Pair Work page 7

Answers will vary.

3 Stative Verbs
Exercise 3.1 Verbs with Stative and Action Meanings

A page 9

2. have	9. think
3. know	10. believes
4. have	11. believe
5. believes	12. get
6. don't seem	13. appear
7. appear	14. believes
8. is having	

B Pair Work page 9

Answers will vary.

Exercise 3.2 Stative or Action Meaning?
page 10

2. do; have	6. don't think
3. is	7. know
4. 'm being	8. 'm having
5. are	9. 're

Exercise 3.3 More Stative or Action Meaning?

A page 11

2. are asking	8. know
3. use	9. looks
4. seem	10. don't think
5. 'm always thinking	11. seems
6. know	12. think
7. am	

B Pair Work page 11

Answers will vary.

4 Special Meanings and Uses of Simple Present

Exercise 4.1 Uses of Simple Present page 12

2. R	5. O
3. O	6. R
4. R	7. P

Exercise 4.2 Summarizing an Article page 13

2. Job candidates sometimes don't/do not tell the truth.
3. A job candidate's score doesn't/does not always reflect the candidate's personality.
4. Candidates who take some personality tests twice sometimes get different scores.
5. These tests don't/do not match people to jobs well.

Exercise 4.3 Giving Instructions

Pair Work page 13

Answers will vary.

5 Avoid Common Mistakes

Editing Task page 14

Without a doubt, first impressions are important.
                              shows
Current research ~~is showing~~ that a first impression can last
                                   is talking
a long time. These days it seems that everyone ~~talks~~ about
the significance of the first 30 seconds of a job interview
                                     believe
or a meeting with a client. However, I ~~am believing~~ there is
another side to this story.
                                have
        Some people ~~are having~~ the ability to make a good first
impression, but the impression may be false. I believe that
                           tell
time and experience ~~are telling~~ the truth about a person's

character. Whenever I talk with someone who smiles at me
                                get
and seems completely charming, I ~~am getting~~ suspicious.
I think that the person is not sincere, and that he or she
wants something from me. On the other hand, I often find
that quieter, more reserved people are more willing to help
me when I ask. My colleague Jim is a good example. This
       working
fall he is ~~work~~ on a special project, so he is very busy, and
sometimes he appears unfriendly. However, he usually
stops and helps me when I ask. My friendlier colleagues
usually smile, but when I ask them for help, they
     make
~~are making~~ excuses.
              don't/do not believe
        In short, I ~~am not believing~~ that everyone who makes
a good first impression deserves my trust. Maybe I am
too suspicious with friendly people, but I will always give
awkward or shy people a second chance. After all, I think
that I may be one of them.

6 Grammar for Writing

Using Simple Present and Present Progressive to Write About Present Time Situations

Pre-writing Task

1 page 15

Possible answer:
Tuesday and Wednesday are the best days.

2 page 15

      Most people (worry) about making a good impression at
a job interview. They generally (think) about what to wear
and what questions to prepare. One thing that people
usually (do not think) about is the day of the appointment.
However, some job experts (believe) that the actual day
makes a difference. For example, some (say) that normally
the worst days (are) Monday and Friday, whereas Tuesday
and Wednesday (are) the best. Monday (is not) ideal because
on that day the interviewer <u>is</u> probably still <u>thinking</u> about
the weekend, and on Friday, the interviewer <u>is</u> usually
<u>watching</u> the clock and <u>waiting</u> for the weekend to start.
On the other hand, Tuesday and Wednesday (are) typically
much better because the interviewer (does not feel) as much
stress as later in the week. There are others who (believe)

that any day is good, but morning appointments (are) better than afternoon ones because interviewers still (feel) relaxed in the morning. People who (want) to have a successful job interview might (want) to choose the right interview day in addition to the perfect outfit.

The writer chose to use the present progressive for *is thinking* and *is watching and waiting* because those actions are in progress at that moment.

Writing Task

1 Write page 15

Answers will vary.

2 Self-Edit page 15

Answers will vary.

2 Simple Past and Past Progressive; *Used To, Would*
Global Marketing

1 Grammar in the Real World

A page 16

Answers will vary; Possible answer: Global-marketing campaigns are successful because they adapt to local cultures.

B Comprehension Check page 17

Possible answers:
1. The doll's image did not appeal to young Chinese women, and they wanted more affordable prices.
2. It was successful because the company adapted its advertising to fit the local culture.
3. Today, successful campaigns depend on understanding the local culture and adapting to the marketing and product to that culture.

C Notice page 17

1. ✓
2.
The verb ends in *-ing*.

2 Simple Past vs. Past Progressive
Exercise 2.1 Simple Past and Past Progressive

A page 18

Benjamin Franklin is one of the fathers of American advertising. He <u>was</u> an early American politician and inventor. In the early 1700s, Franklin <u>was working</u> in Philadelphia, Pennsylvania, as a publisher and inventor. He <u>published</u> a variety of books, and he <u>was</u> also the publisher of the newspaper *The Pennsylvania Gazette*. He <u>used</u> *The Pennsylvania Gazette* to advertise his inventions. Franklin <u>filled</u> the newspaper with ads. He also <u>advertised</u> books, both his own and other people's. Because of the ads in his newspaper, Franklin <u>was making</u> a lot of money and <u>was selling</u> a lot of books. These <u>were</u> among the first advertisements in America.

B Pair Work page 18

Simple past: was, published, was, used, filled, advertised, were
Past progressive: was working, was making, was selling

Exercise 2.2 Simple Past or Past Progressive?

A page 19

2. were soon drinking
3. wasn't working
4. were going
5. decided
6. learned
7. hired
8. designed
9. became
10. increased / were increasing

B Pair Work page 19

Answers will vary.

3 Time Clauses with Simple Past and Past Progressive
Exercise 3.1 Time Clauses with *After*, *Before*, *Once*, and *When* pages 21–22

2. People drank more milk than soft drinks (before) ¹ soft-drink companies started marketing their drinks ² as "fun."

3. (When) soft-drink companies began marketing their ¹ drinks as "fun," the California Milk Advisory Board ² (CMAB) realized it needed to market milk differently.

4. The CMAB learned that people thought milk was boring ² (after) the board completed its market research. ¹

5. (When) the CMAB discovered that 70 percent of ¹ Californians already drank milk, it decided to create a ² campaign to persuade them to drink more milk.

6. (Before) it started a new ad campaign, the new California ² ¹ Milk Processor Board, MilkPEP, learned that most

people drink milk at home with foods like cookies and cake.

7. (When) the new milk ads appeared,^{1} they^2 immediately became famous.

8. MilkPEP created a successful^2 Spanish-language milk ad (once) it had success with the "Got milk?" campaign.^{1}

Exercise 3.2 Time Clauses with *As Soon As*, *Before*, *Until*, and *While* pages 22–23

2. While Europeans were exploring the world from the fifteenth to the seventeenth centuries, they found new and interesting kinds of food and spices. *OR* Europeans found new and interesting kinds of food and spices while they were exploring the world from the fifteenth to the seventeenth centuries.
3. As soon as European explorers came home, they introduced the items to the people from their countries. *OR* European explorers introduced the items to the people from their countries as soon as they came home.
4. Europeans didn't know anything about coffee before they read the ads that explained what it was. *OR* Before Europeans read the ads that explained what coffee was, Europeans didn't know anything about it.
5. Early advertisements had no words because most people couldn't read until literacy became widespread in the eighteenth century. *OR* Until literacy became widespread in the eighteenth century, early advertisements had no words because most people couldn't read.
6. Newspapers were the most common form of advertising before radio was invented in the 1920s. *OR* Before radio was invented in the 1920s, newspapers were the most common form of advertising.

Exercise 3.3 Using Time Clauses with *When* and *While* page 23

2. was considering; realized
3. were doing; decided
4. learned; were interviewing
5. were listening; got
6. was thinking; learned
7. were contemplating; became

Exercise 3.4 More Using Time Clauses with *When* and *While*

A Over to You page 24

Answers will vary.

B Pair Work page 24

Answers will vary.

4 *Used To* and *Would*

Exercise 4.1 *Would* pages 25–26

2. would appear
3. wouldn't/would not use
4. would read
5. would buy
6. would create
7. would match
8. would advertise

Exercise 4.2 *Used To*, *Would*, or Simple Past?

A page 26

2. used to tell
3. used to be
4. didn't use to try
5. would; create
6. would say
7. would show
8. didn't use to hide
9. saw
10. showed
11. decided

B page 26

Same as **A**.

Exercise 4.3 Using *Used To*, *Would*, and Simple Past

Group Work page 27

Answers will vary.

5 Avoid Common Mistakes

Editing Task page 28

Hello, everyone! Welcome to the meeting.
                                         was
As many of you know, this past year ^disappointing for

many companies. However, we ended up doing quite well

here at ABC Cell Phones. At the beginning of the year,
        were   *were falling*
things ^looking bad. In fact, our sales ~~fell~~ when I started

here. However, our excellent marketing team did their
                    created
research, and they ~~create~~ new and extremely successful
                         discovered
advertisements after they ~~discover~~ two shifts in consumer

spending.

   The first shift they saw was a shift to green marketing.
                                              pay
Last year we noticed that consumers would ~~paid~~ more

for environmentally friendly products. Therefore, our first

advertisement of last year showed how good our cell phone batteries are for the environment.

The second shift was in who advertised our products.
were writing
While we ~~wrote~~ our most recent advertisement, research arrived that showed that celebrities sell products better. In October we began showing famous actors and actresses *rose* using our phones, and last month alone, our sales ~~rise~~ by 25 percent.

In short, while some businesses were struggling,
were
we ⌃increasing our profits.

6 Grammar for Writing
Using Past and Present Forms to Write About Changes

Pre-writing Task

1 page 29

Possible answers:
Advertisers used to use jingles. Advertisers are starting to use jingles again these days.

2 page 29

Music in advertising has gone through different stages throughout the years. In the 1950s and 1960s, every product <u>used to have</u> a jingle, a short piece of music that is appealing and singable. A product (would have) several different advertisements, but the jingle <u>was</u> always the same. Jingles <u>used to be</u> effective because consumers (would sing) them at different times to themselves, and the songs (would remind) them about the product. In the 1980s, advertisers <u>stopped</u> using jingles and <u>started</u> using hit songs. Nike <u>was</u> the first to do this. It successfully <u>used</u> the Beatles's song "Revolution" in its advertisements. Other companies <u>followed</u> Nike. Today, an interesting thing is happening. Companies are creating jingles for their products again. However, the jingles of today are different because they have to compete with the short, snappy songs on MP3 players and the songs used as ringtones. They simply don't stand out as being different from regular songs anymore.

Writing Task

1 Write page 29

Answers will vary.

2 Self-Edit page 29

Answers will vary.

3 Present Perfect and Present Perfect Progressive
Success

1 Grammar in the Real World

A page 30

Answers will vary; Possible answer: both Mahatma Gandhi and Bill Gates had a purpose in life and were not afraid to take action, to take risks, or to work hard.

B Comprehension Check page 31

Possible answers:
1. Mahatma Gandhi supported nonviolence.
2. It contributes money to organizations and programs working in global health.
3. They have found a purpose in life and are not afraid to take action, to take risks, or to work hard.

C Notice page 31

1. c   2. c   3. a

Verbs that describe actions that are still happening now: have been inspiring, has been guiding

2 Present Perfect
Exercise 2.1 Uses of Present Perfect page 33

Blake Mycoskie is an American businessperson. He started a shoe company called TOMS in 2006. He sells a special type of shoe, the alpargata. He discovered the shoe
C
in Argentina. Argentinean farmers **have worn** alpargatas for over 100 years.

R
Recently, experts **have discovered** a link between children going barefoot and getting certain diseases.
C
Mycoskie **has** always **wanted** to help children stay healthy. Therefore, every time someone buys a pair of TOMS shoes, his company gives a free pair of new shoes to a child who
C
needs shoes. Since he started TOMS, Mycoskie **has given** over a million pairs of alpargatas to children in South Africa, Ethiopia, Rwanda, Argentina, Guatemala, Haiti, and the United States.

Not long ago, Mycoskie **started** (U) a shoe factory in Ethiopia. He **has** also **created** (U) a special shoe that helps prevent a serious foot disease. Mycoskie's favorite quote comes from Gandhi: "Be the change you wish to see in the world."

Exercise 2.2 Using Present Perfect

A page 34

2. 's achieved
3. 's had
4. have; known
5. 've known
6. Has; been
7. 's been
8. haven't had
9. 've raised
10. has; graduated
11. has; gotten
12. 've; thought
13. haven't achieved

B Group Work page 35

Answers will vary.

Exercise 2.3 *For* or *Since*? page 35

2. for
3. since
4. for
5. For

Exercise 2.4 More *For* or *Since*? page 35

2. They have had only one fight since they first met.
3. They haven't/have not spent a night apart since 1980.
4. They have been friends since high school.
5. They have spoken on the phone every day for the past 10 years.
6. Verónica has been a successful single parent for many years.
7. She has raised her three children by herself since her divorce.

3 Present Perfect vs. Simple Past
Exercise 3.1 Present Perfect or Simple Past?

A page 37

2. Did she use
3. did
4. played
5. 's performed
6. played
7. has she done
8. produced
9. 's been
10. was
11. had

B Pair Work page 38

Answers will vary.

Exercise 3.2 More Present Perfect or Simple Past?

A page 38

2. Diane/she moved to Florida. She studied English at a school for fashion design
3. Diane/she finished college. She worked as a seamstress in Miami
4. Diane/she moved to New York. She got a job at Smith Designs
5. Diane/she became a designer at Smith Designs
6. Diane/she left Smith Designs. She started a company, Sorel Designs
7. Diane/she has worked at Sorel Designs
8. Diane/she has made movie costumes

B Over to You page 38

Answers will vary.

4 Present Perfect vs. Present Perfect Progressive
Exercise 4.1 Completed or Ongoing Actions? page 40

	Completed	Ongoing
2.	☐	☑
3.	☐	☑
4.	☐	☑
5.	☐	☑
6.	☑	☐
7.	☐	☑
8.	☑	☐
9.	☐	☑
10.	☑	☐
11.	☐	☑
12.	☐	☑
13.	☐	☑
14.	☑	☐

Exercise 4.2 Simple Past, Present Perfect, and Present Perfect Progressive

A page 41

2. studied
3. has worked / has been working
4. has taught / has been teaching
5. had
6. left
7. started
8. opened
9. has started

B Pair Work page 41

Answers will vary.

C page 41

Same as **A**.

D Over to You page 42

Answers will vary.

5 Avoid Common Mistakes

Editing Task pages 42–43

    I am a college student by day and a sous-chef by night.

                                        has

My studies are important, but my restaurant job ~~have~~

                                               have been

taught me what I really need to know about success. I ~~am~~

working in the kitchen of Da Lat, a French-Vietnamese

bistro, for three years, and the job has been a wonderful

experience for me because I have learned many new skills.

               become

    First, I have ~~been becoming~~ a much better planner since

I started working at Da Lat. Planning and preparation are

                             has

very important in a kitchen. If the chef ~~have~~ not prepared

the ingredients well beforehand, it will take too long to

make each dish, and customers will complain. We start

our preparation early each day, and by the time the first

                            been

customer comes, we have ˄working for 6 hours.

                been

    Second, I have ˄developing better interpersonal skills.

                     received

For example, I have ~~been receiving~~ two promotions in the

last two years. Last year, I became a line cook because I had

learned to pay attention to what others might need before

                                 have been

they ask. I think that for the past few months, I ~~am~~ paying

better attention in other areas of my life as well.

    My college education is important, but I will always be

                             has

grateful for my job at Da Lat. This job ~~have~~ given me mental

and social skills for my future.

6 Grammar for Writing

Using Present Perfect, Present Perfect Progressive, and Simple Past to Describe a Series of Events

Pre-writing Task

1 page 44

Possible answers:

She won a national competition to design the Vietnam Veterans Memorial. Lin was just 21 years old and still an undergraduate in college at that time. She has been designing monuments, parks, and other important structures ever since.

2 page 44

    Maya Lin is an incredible American architect and artist. Her career (began) when she (won) a national competition to design the Vietnam Veterans Memorial in 1981. Lin (was) just 21 years old and (was) still an undergraduate in college at that time. This memorial (became) famous almost immediately. Millions of people <u>have traveled</u> to Washington, D.C., to see it over the years. Since then, Lin <u>has accomplished</u> many more things. She (completed) her master's in architecture in 1986, and she <u>has been designing</u> monuments, parks, and other important structures ever since. She <u>has designed</u> many of her structures to draw people's attention to nature, to the environment, and to social issues. Recently she <u>has been creating</u> a lot of landscape art. Because Lin is both an artist and an architect, she combines both of her interests in her designs. People <u>have been questioning</u> whether her work is art or architecture for many years. Lin likes to think of her work as a combination of both. Lin <u>has won</u> awards and honorary degrees throughout her career. Not all of Lin's designs <u>have been</u> popular, but Maya Lin <u>has been</u> a very successful architect and artist since she (was) a very young woman.

Writing Task

1 Write page 44

Answers will vary.

2 Self-Edit page 45

Answers will vary.

4 Past Perfect and Past Perfect Progressive
Nature vs. Nurture

1 Grammar in the Real World

A page 46

Answers will vary; Possible answer: They were surprised by their many similarities.

B Comprehension Check page 47

Possible answers:
1. They were part of a secret study; neither family knew the girls were twins.
2. They looked almost identical, they had both studied film, and they both loved to write.
3. It is an argument over whether nature (genetics) or nurture (the environment) has a greater impact on the development of an individual.

C Notice page 47

1. Both girls <u>knew</u> that their parents <u>had adopted</u> them as infants.
2. She <u>had been doing</u> research on her birth mother when she <u>made</u> a surprising discovery.
3. Even more surprising, she <u>learned</u> that she <u>had been</u> part of a secret scientific study.
1. had adopted; knew
2. had been doing; made
3. had been; learned

The verb that happened first starts with *had*. The verb that happened second is in the simple past.

2 Past Perfect
Exercise 2.1 Past Perfect page 49

2. had lived
3. had gone
4. hadn't/had not gone; hadn't/had not attended
5. had married
6. had gotten; had remarried; hadn't/had not gotten
7. had; owned
8. had given
9. had; worked
10. had worked; hadn't/had not worked; had been

Exercise 2.2 Past Perfect and Simple Past

A page 50

The University of Minnesota is the birthplace of one of the most important twin studies in the world. It <u>started</u> in 1979. Thomas J. Bouchard <u>had</u> already <u>been</u> on the faculty of the university for some time when he <u>began</u> his study of identical twins. Bouchard <u>read</u> an article about a set of twins who <u>had been</u> separated at birth. The twins <u>had</u> recently <u>met</u> and <u>had found</u> many similarities. They <u>found out</u> that they <u>had lived</u> near each other for years. Bouchard <u>was</u> amazed by the twins' story and <u>decided</u> to start the Minnesota Twins Reared Apart Study. Bouchard <u>began</u> to study sets of twins that <u>had been</u> separated at birth. Over the years, the Minnesota Twins Reared Apart Study <u>has studied</u> more than 8,000 sets of twins. The study continues today.

B Pair Work page 50

Answers will vary.

Exercise 2.3 More Past Perfect and Simple Past

A pages 50–51

2. told
3. hadn't done
4. decided
5. saw
6. had shown up
7. had; worn
8. had; started
9. returned
10. Had; read
11. had come out
12. went
13. hadn't been

B page 51

Same as **A**.

C page 52

2. hadn't/had not recorded
3. had decided
4. hadn't/had not started
5. had graduated
6. had built

D Over to You page 52

Answers will vary.

3 Past Perfect with Time Clauses
Exercise 3.1 Order of Events

A page 53

Before her twins were born, Kim Lee <u>had read</u> a lot about twin studies. After she <u>had done</u> a little research, Kim found an early reading study for twins. She contacted the researchers and learned that she had to wait until the twins were four years old. When she enrolled the twins in the study, she <u>hadn't known</u> that the twins needed to give a DNA sample. As soon as Kim learned this, she took the twins out of the study. Kim thought that taking a DNA sample was an invasion of her children's privacy.

B Pair Work page 54

Answers will vary.

Exercise 3.2 Time Clauses page 54

3. Before
4. knew / had known
5. As soon as
6. discovered / had discovered
7. After
8. found / had found
9. Until
10. hadn't / had not known
11. As soon as
12. discovered / had discovered
13. Before
14. met / had met

Exercise 3.3 Combining Sentences page 55

Possible answers:

2. Diego and Shannon had not thought much about the nature versus nurture debate until their first child, Mario, was born.
3. Before they became parents, Diego and Shannon hadn't had much experience with music.
4. After three-year-old Mario had seen an electronic keyboard in a shop, he asked his parents to buy him one.
5. As soon as Diego and Shannon had heard Mario playing the keyboard, they realized their son's musical talent.
6. As soon as Diego and Shannon had realized Mario's talent, they enrolled him in piano classes.
7. Mario became an excellent musician after Diego and Shannon had enrolled Mario in piano classes.
8. By the time Mario had taken a few years of piano classes, he started composing music.

4 Past Perfect Progressive

Exercise 4.1 Past Perfect Progressive page 57

2. hadn't / had not been working
3. had been making
4. had been selling
5. had been interviewing
6. had been talking
7. had been doing
8. hadn't / had not been living
9. had been crossing

Exercise 4.2 Past Perfect Progressive, Past Perfect, or Simple Past?

A page 58

2. hadn't been having / hadn't had
3. had adopted
4. 'd been talking

5. 'd been searching
6. met
7. 'd been looking
8. 'd been speaking / 'd spoken / spoke
9. 'd been looking / 'd looked

B Pair Work page 58

Either the past perfect or the past perfect progressive: 2, 8, 9
Only the past perfect: 3

C Over to You page 58

Answers will vary.

5 Avoid Common Mistakes

Editing Task page 59

I ~~have~~ *had* never really thought about sibling differences until my own children were born. When we had our first child, my husband and I ~~have~~ *had* lived in Chicago for just a few months. We ~~have~~ *had* not made many friends yet, so we spent all our time with our child. Baby Gilbert was happy to be the center of attention. He depended on us for everything.

By the time our second son, Chase, was born, we ~~have~~ *had* developed a community of friends and a busier social life. We frequently visited friends and left the children at home with a babysitter. As a result of our busy schedules, Chase was more independent. One day I had just ~~been hanging~~ *hung* up the phone when Chase came into the room. Chase picked up the phone and started talking into it. I thought he was pretending, but I was wrong. He had ~~been figuring~~ *figured* out how to use the phone!

When my husband came home, he was tired because he ~~worked~~ *had worked / had been working* all day. When I told him about Chase's phone conversation, though, he became very excited. Gilbert ~~has~~ *had* never used the phone as a child. At first, we were surprised that Chase was so different from Gilbert. Then we realized that because of our busy lifestyles, Chase had learned to be independent.

6 Grammar for Writing
Using Past Perfect to Provide Background Information and Reasons

Pre-writing Task

1 page 60

Possible answers:
He believes that the experiences that a person has outside the home can be as influential as the experiences inside the home.

2 page 60

I believe that the experiences that a person has outside the home can be as influential as experiences inside the home. Examples of this are siblings who start out very similar but become very different from one another as they grow older. For example, Andy and Frank are two brothers who are only two years apart. They did everything together and were best friends (until they started junior high). (After Andy had been in seventh grade for a little while,) he started to change. He had made new friends at school, so he and Frank did not see each other much during the day. Frank had made new friends, too. In fact, Andy's new friends did not like Frank very much, so Andy did not feel comfortable asking Frank to spend time with them. (By the time Andy and Frank were in high school,) they had grown very far apart. They had made different friends and they had developed different interests. They had been similar (when they were young,) but Andy and Frank had very little in common as young adults.

Writing Task

1 Write page 61

Answers will vary.

2 Self-Edit page 61

Answers will vary.

5 *Be Going To*, Present Progressive, and Future Progressive
Looking Ahead at Technology

1 Grammar in the Real World

A page 62

Answers will vary; Possible answer: One way technology will change is through the development of fabric-based computers.

B Comprehension Check page 63

Possible answers:
1. The world will be blanketed by Wi-Fi; computers will be combined with watches, glasses, shirts, or backpacks; and other people will use smart clothing.
2. They will access the Internet through glasses or clothing.
3. "Smart clothing" is technology which combines computers with clothing.

C Notice page 63

1. will be depending
2. is going to become
3. will use
There are three different verb forms.

2 *Be Going To*, Present Progressive, and Simple Present for Future
Exercise 2.1 *Be Going To* or Present Progressive?

A page 64

2. is having *OR* is going to have
3. are lowering *OR* are going to lower
4. 'm/am visiting
5. are going to give
6. 'm/am meeting *OR* 'm/am going to meet
7. are; doing *OR* are; going to do
8. 'm/am going *OR* 'm/am going to go

B Pair Work page 64

Answers will vary.

Exercise 2.2 *Be Going To*, Present Progressive, or Simple Present? page 65

2. becomes
3. are preparing
4. are opening
5. are giving
6. closes
7. is going to interview
8. is; going to speak

Exercise 2.3 More *Be Going To*, Present Progressive, or Simple Present?

A page 66

2. is; going to start
3. is going to put
4. is going to show
5. are going to meet / are meeting / meet
6. are planning / plan
7. is going / goes

B Pair Work page 66

Answers will vary.

3 *Will* and *Be Going To*

Exercise 3.1 *Will* or *Be Going To*?

A page 68

2. Will you
3. will
4. 'll
5. will you
6. will
7. 'll *OR* 'm going to
8. 'll *OR* 'm going to

B Pair Work   page 68

Answers will vary.

Exercise 3.2 More *Will* or *Be Going To*?

A page 69

2. is going to make
3. will; open
4. 'll do
5. will; turn off
6. won't ask
7. 're going to hear
8. will; find
9. is going to be
10. will offer
11. will save
12. will save
13. will use
14. will; be

B page 69

a request: 1, 3, 5
a prediction based on evidence: 2, 7, 9
a promise: 6, 8
an offer: 4

C Group Work   page 69

Answers will vary.

4 Future Progressive

Exercise 4.1 Future Progressive   page 71

2. will be saving
3. won't/will not be buying
4. will be watching
5. will be using
6. won't/will not be watching
7. will be socializing
8. will be sending
9. will be chatting
10. will be asking

Exercise 4.2 Future Progressive or *Be Going To*?

A page 72

2. Are; going to be watching *OR* Will; be watching
3. Are; going to be viewing *OR* Will; be viewing
4. is going to be discussing *OR* will be discussing
5. is going to be giving *OR* will be giving
6. is going to be taking *OR* will be taking

B page 72

2. 'm/am; going to attend *OR* 'm/am; going to be attending *OR* will; be attending

3. 'm/am not going to go *OR* 'm/am not going to be going *OR* won't/will not be going
4. are; going to go *OR* are; going to be going *OR* will; be going
5. 'm/am going to take *OR* 'm/am going to be taking *OR* will be taking
6. 'm/am; going to ask *OR* 'm/am; going to be asking *OR* will; be asking

Exercise 4.3 More Future Progressive

Over to You   page 72

Answers will vary.

5 Avoid Common Mistakes

Editing Task   page 73

Hi Layla,

Thanks for agreeing to take this trip on short notice.
Vinh can't go because he'll ~~present~~ *be presenting* at a conference in Chicago, and your name came up immediately as a replacement. We know you are familiar with the software, so we feel confident that you ^*are* going to do a great job.

Your first flight leaves Newark Liberty International Airport at 9:00 a.m. on the twenty-second and arrives in London late in the afternoon. That evening you are having dinner with James and Eleanor Wilson. They ^*are* going to be driving you around during your stay.

On Monday, your first presentation starts at 9:00 a.m. at the headquarters of Logan and Lowe. We have scheduled three presentations that day. You are going to be very busy!

You leave London on the 8:00 p.m. flight to Beijing. In Beijing you won't have much free time because you ~~will give~~ *will be giving* your presentation at several companies. Alan ^*is* ~~going~~ to send you the details in a separate e-mail. You ~~are~~ *will be* flying when he sends it.

Best of luck,

Antoine

6 Grammar for Writing
Using *Will* + Base Form and Future Progressive to Write About Future Plans

Pre-writing Task

1 page 74

Possible answer:
Ms. Gabriel is changing all the classrooms into smart classrooms.

2 page 74

Claire Gabriel, director of the Hillspoint College Language Center, <u>will be making</u> some exciting changes to the college's Language Center (LC) classrooms over the next two years. First, Ms. Gabriel <u>will be transforming</u> all the classrooms into smart classrooms. Each room (will have) computers, projectors, and an Internet connection. Teachers and students (will be able to access) the Internet at any time. They (will work) with students and teachers all over the world using video conferencing. Next, Ms. Gabriel <u>will be installing</u> moveable walls. These walls (will allow) teachers to change one classroom into several small classrooms with the touch of a button. This (will be) useful when students are working in groups. Toward the end of the two-year period, Ms. Gabriel <u>will be making</u> more changes. She (will purchase) smart desks with touch screens for students. Touch screens (will allow) students to take part in interactive activities. Several students (will be able to do) an activity together at the same time. According to Ms. Gabriel, the touch screens (will encourage) even shy students to participate in class. Surprisingly, all these changes (will not increase) student fees. The money for the upgrades (will come) from generous members of the Hillspoint community.

The main ideas introduce the steps: Ms. Gabriel makes changes; first, she will transform classrooms into smart classrooms; next, she will install moveable walls; toward the end, she will make more changes

Writing Task

1 Write page 75

Answers will vary.

2 Self-Edit page 75

Answers will vary.

6 Future Time Clauses, Future Perfect, and Future Perfect Progressive
Business Practices of the Future

1 Grammar in the Real World

A page 76

Answers will vary; Possible answer: The pros to cloud computing include cutting costs and attracting more customers. The cons include decreased security.

B Comprehension Check page 77

Possible answers:
1. Technology departments won't exist in the future because companies won't need them when they have access to the cloud.
2. Cloud services may not be secure. There is a growing number of hacking attempts.

C Notice page 77

1. will have eliminated; will have been using
2. will not use

Completed future event: will have eliminated

2 Future Time Clauses
Exercise 2.1 Using Future Time Clauses

A page 79

2. <u>Companies will start saving a great deal of money</u> (as soon as) they move their work to the cloud.
3. <u>Companies are going to have difficulty competing</u> (until) they begin advertising on social networking sites.
4. (After) companies have moved to cloud computing, <u>they will receive technological support and updates on new technology.</u>
5. (Once) companies believe that the data is secure with cloud services, <u>more companies are going to move their data to the cloud.</u>

B pages 79–80

2. will not be; begin
3. starts; are going to save
4. are going to save; have changed
5. isn't going to save; become
6. has created; will have
7. won't approve; has approved

Exercise 2.2 Time Clauses with *When* and *While* pages 80–81

2. 're/are finding OR find
3. 're/are doing
4. is working
5. 'm/am studying OR study
6. 'm/am looking
7. 're/are analyzing
8. 're/are thinking

Exercise 2.3 Time Clauses with *When* page 81

2. will introduce
3. will photocopy
4. will hand out
5. will put
6. will be walking; (will be) taking OR will walk; (will) take
7. will be finishing OR will finish
8. will reassemble

Exercise 2.4 More Future Time Clauses

A page 82

Possible answers:

2. Until Marta and Aaron have gotten business training, they won't get management training.
3. After Aaron has thought of a name for the business, Marta will find a location for the business.
4. Marta and Aaron will buy equipment for the business after Marta has gotten a tax identification number.
5. Marta and Aaron will open the business after they have promoted the business.
6. They will close for one week after they have had a sale.

B Pair Work page 82

Answers will vary.

3 Future Perfect vs. Future Perfect Progressive

Exercise 3.1 Future Perfect page 84

2. will have started
3. won't/will not have arrived
4. will have ended
5. will have gone out to eat lunch
6. won't/will not have returned from lunch
7. will have arrived home
8. will have left work
9. won't/will not have eaten dinner

Exercise 3.2 Future Perfect Progressive page 85

2. By 4:00 on Tuesday, Eric will have been discussing the new project for three hours.
3. By 6:45 on Tuesday, Eric will have been talking on the phone for half an hour.
4. By 4:00 on Wednesday, Eric will have been attending a software training for seven hours.
5. By 5:00 on Friday, Eric will have been attending a software training for three days.
6. By 7:15 on Friday, Eric will have been working out at the gym for 75 minutes.

Exercise 3.3 Time Clauses with Future Perfect and Future Perfect Progressive

A page 86

2. Yes
3. No
4. No
5. Yes
6. No
7. Yes
8. No

B page 86

Same as **A**.

C Over to You page 86

Answers will vary.

4 Avoid Common Mistakes

Editing Task page 87

Experts say that by 2020, the health-care industry
have changed
will ~~change~~ in many ways because of technology and the Internet. I plan on working in this industry, so it is fascinating for me to know that by the time I graduate,
will have
the job market ~~has~~ changed dramatically. One change that interests me is in the doctor-patient relationship. By
have empowered
that time, technology will ~~empower~~ patients because they
using
will have been ~~used~~ the Internet to gather information and discuss information with others. Also, health-care
using
companies will have been ~~used~~ cloud computing for a few years, so a patient's medical files will always be available to both the patient and the doctor. This means that, for
arrives
example, when a patient ~~will arrive~~ for his appointment,
will
he will not have to fill out forms, and the doctor ⌃ have already seen the patient's information. By the time a patient decides on a treatment, the doctor and patient will have ~~been~~ discussed many options. The whole health-care system will have improved, so more people will live in a state of health.

5 Grammar for Writing
Using Future Perfect and Future Perfect Progressive to Write About Completed and Ongoing Events in the Future

Pre-writing Task

1 pages 88–89

Possible answers:

The writer is probably an employee of Westport City College. You could find a similar paragraph in a brochure or on a website.

2 page 89

    Westport City College (WCC) has become a well-respected institution in the Westport community over the past several decades. <u>By the end of this spring</u>, WCC <u>will have been educating</u> students for 50 years. <u>Once summer break begins</u>, we (will have served) over 1 million Westport residents. WCC has always offered programs in leading fields of industry, and we are constantly updating our programs to teach the most up-to-date information. Right now, we have exciting news for students with an interest in computers. <u>By next fall</u>, WCC <u>will have been offering</u> a certificate program in Information Technology for over 30 years, but we are planning many important changes to the program for September. For example, we will offer a specialized certificate in cloud computing next fall. Two new professors will be joining our team of excellent instructors to help make this happen. Professor Gordon Jones will be teaching several basic courses, including Cloud Computing 101. <u>By the time he joins us</u>, Professor Jones <u>will have been working</u> in cloud computing for 10 years. Professor Margaret Chan (will have trained) employees to use cloud computing in over a dozen successful technology companies <u>by the time she begins</u> teaching at WCC. If you are interested in enrolling in our new and improved IT certificate program, please send your application right away. A lot of students are interested, and at this rate, we (will have received) over 200 applications <u>by the end of the month</u>!

Actions which will be completed in the future: future perfect
Actions which will be ongoing in the future: future perfect progressive
Expressions followed by a time or noun clause: by
Expressions followed by a clause: by the time

Writing Task

1 Write page 89

Answers will vary.

2 Self-Edit page 89

Answers will vary.

7 Social Modals
Learning How to Remember

1 Grammar in the Real World

A page 90

Answers will vary.

B Comprehension Check page 91

Possible answers:
1. To remember something, you must pay attention.
2. Visualization is creating a mental picture of what you want to remember.
3. Some ways to exercise your brain include tackling the daily crossword puzzle, changing a daily routine, writing with your nondominant hand, and taking a different route to school or work.

C Notice page 91

1. have to
2. should have
3. have to
Necessary to do something: 1, 3

2 Modals and Modal-like Expressions of Advice and Regret
Exercise 2.1 Present and Future Advice

A page 93

2. could   4. shouldn't
3. might   5. should

B Pair Work page 93

Answers will vary.

Exercise 2.2 More Present and Future Advice

A page 94

Hi *Answers will vary*,
2. You ought to read your textbook two or three times.
3. You might try teaching someone else the material.
4. You shouldn't/should not wait until the last minute to study.
5. You'd/You had better get plenty of sleep before a test.
Best,

Answers will vary

B Pair Work page 94

Answers will vary.

Exercise 2.3 Past Advice and Regret

A page 95

2. should have taken
3. ought to have summarized
4. should have given
5. ought to have started
6. shouldn't/should not have waited
7. should have talked
8. should have helped

B Pair Work page 95

Answers will vary.

C Group Work page 95

Answers will vary.

3 Modals and Modal-like Expressions of Permission, Necessity, and Obligation

Exercise 3.1 Present and Future Permission

A page 97

2. may not use
3. can use
4. aren't/are not allowed to access
5. are allowed to bring
6. must not use
7. may not use

B page 98

2. He isn't/is not allowed to use an online dictionary during a test.
3. She may use a print dictionary during tests.
4. She can bring a laptop to class.
5. He isn't/is not permitted to check his e-mail on his laptop during class.
6. He can't/cannot go to the lab.

Exercise 3.2 Past Permission

A page 98

2. couldn't/could not use
3. were permitted to bring
4. weren't/were not allowed to browse
5. were allowed to go
6. Were; allowed to speak
7. weren't/were not allowed to do

B Over to You page 98

Answers will vary.

Exercise 3.3 Present and Future Necessity and Obligation page 99

2. You must not be afraid to ask questions in class.
3. You're/You are supposed to turn in all your homework.
4. You must bring a flash drive next week.
5. You're/You are required to write an essay at the end of the semester.
6. You aren't/are not supposed to text during class.
7. You don't/do not need to send your writing assignments electronically.

Exercise 3.4 More Present and Future Necessity and Obligation

A page 99

2. D	6. D
3. D	7. D
4. S	8. S
5. S	

B page 99

Same as **A**.

Exercise 3.5 Past Necessity and Obligation

A page 100

2. had to work
3. had to take
4. was required to read
5. wasn't/was not supposed to miss
6. had to attend
7. had to go

B Over to You page 100

Answers will vary.

4 Modals and Modal-like Expressions of Ability

Exercise 4.1 Past, Present, and Future Ability pages 101–102

2. could ride
3. 's/is able to do
4. won't/will not be able to return
5. 'll/will be able to take care

Exercise 4.2 Past Ability page 102

2. could have made
3. couldn't/could not have imagined
4. couldn't/could not have remembered
5. could have managed

5 Avoid Common Mistakes

Editing Task page 103

    Technology *is* supposed to simplify life; however, in reality,
it has led to people trying to do too many things at once.
One example is driving while texting or talking on a cell
phone. After an accident, drivers who are caught by
the police admit that they should *have* turned off their
phones when they got in the car, but they did not. They
~~must not have called~~ *did not have to call* someone while driving, but they did.

    Another issue is multitasking in the classroom. Many
of my teachers have had a difficult time dealing with
students who surf the Web while listening to lectures. One
of my instructors said he ought to *have* required a password last
semester to log onto the Internet during class. Students
~~must not have gone~~ *did not have to go* online, but they sometimes checked
e-mail or visited websites instead of listening to the lecture.
As a result, students were often distracted.

    In contrast, my friend had an instructor who had the
opposite view. My friend did not worry about taking
notes because students *were* not allowed to – even on paper!
The professor thought all note taking was a form of
multitasking; instead, he handed out worksheets with
highlights of his lecture. At the end of the semester, some
students complained. They argued that the professor
should not *have* banned computers in class because students
today are used to multitasking.

6 Grammar for Writing
Using Modals to Write About Problems and Solutions

Pre-writing Task

1 page 104

Possible answers:
Stress can lead to poor test scores. The writer suggests that
colleges and universities should address this problem in
their new-student orientations and provide stress reduction
workshops for students throughout the school year.

2 page 104

    Research shows a strong relationship between high
levels of stress and low levels of academic achievement.
Stress causes the body to produce high levels of the
hormone cortisol. This hormone <u>can limit</u> the brain's ability
to process information. Therefore, high levels of stress
<u>can have</u> a negative effect on memory and <u>could lead</u> to
poor test scores. For this reason, colleges and universities
<u>should address</u> the problems of stress in their new-student
orientations. First, they <u>should teach</u> new students to
recognize the signs of stress, such as headaches, anxiety,
and trouble sleeping. The orientation schedule <u>might
include</u> relaxation classes and deep-breathing lessons.
Counselors <u>could</u> also <u>tell</u> students about the importance
of exercise. In addition, colleges and universities <u>should
provide</u> stress reduction workshops for students during the
school year. Students who learn how to manage their stress
will remember what they learn, and will therefore have a
better chance at success in their studies.

Writing Task

1 Write page 105
Answers will vary.

2 Self-Edit page 105
Answers will vary.

8 Modals of Probability: Present, Future, and Past
Computers and Crime

1 Grammar in the Real World

A page 106

Answers will vary; Possible answer: Some ways to prevent
hackers include using antivirus software and using
complex passwords.

B Comprehension Check page 107

Possible answers:
1. Many hackers are teenagers.
2. Some hackers steal credit card numbers and other
   personal information
3. No one's computer is completely safe from hackers.

C Notice page 107

	Possible	Very Certain
1.	✔	☐
2.	✔	☐
3.	☐	✔
4.	☐	✔

Words that tell an action or situation is possible: can, might

2 Modals of Present Probability

Exercise 2.1 Present Probability

A pages 108–109

2. must *OR* have to
3. must *OR* has to
4. can't/cannot *OR* couldn't/could not
5. must *OR* have to
6. should *OR* ought to
7. can't/cannot *OR* couldn't/could not
8. could *OR* may *OR* might

B Pair Work page 109

Answers will vary.

Exercise 2.2 More Present Probability

A Over to You pages 109–110

Answers will vary.

B Pair Work page 110

No answers.

3 Modals of Future Probability

Exercise 3.1 Future Probability

A page 111

2. will be	5. will allow
3. won't/will not need	6. will lock
4. will let	7. will be

B page 112

2. should	5. won't
3. may not	6. ought to
4. could	

C Pair Work page 112

Answers will vary.

Exercise 3.2 More Future Probability

A page 112–113

2. They may not	6. I could
3. They might not	7. They should
4. He may	8. they could
5. That might	9. It'll

B page 113

Same as **A.**

4 Modals of Past Probability

Exercise 4.1 Past Probability page 115

2. couldn't/could not have been
3. must have obtained
4. could; have happened
5. might have stolen
6. may have stolen
7. could have taken

Exercise 4.2 More Past Probability page 115

2. Someone must have stolen his credit card number.
3. He must not have called the credit card company
4. He may/might/could have copied the card number.
5. She must not have thought it was important.

Exercise 4.3 Using Modals of Past Probability page 116

Possible answers:
2. She must not have checked her credit card bill for incorrect charges.
3. He must have carried all of his credit cards with him.
4. He must not have made a photocopy of his passport.
5. She must have given out personal information.

5 Avoid Common Mistakes

Editing Task page 117

What happens to computer hackers who decide to stop hacking? They might find that cyber crime can lead to interesting careers. For example, some companies hire a computer hacker with the hope that the former cyber criminal ~~must~~ *will* become a brilliant security consultant in the future. Although some say that these companies might *be* taking a risk by hiring these former criminals, the companies seem to believe that the risk is worth it. Adrian Lamo was breaking into computer systems for fun in high school. However, when he hacked into the *New York Times* in 2002, the newspaper must *not* have ~~not~~ thought it was funny, because he was arrested. He now uses his skills for a different purpose and works as a consultant. Robert Tappan Morris might have ended his chances for a good job when he created the Morris worm, a particularly bad computer virus, in 1988. However, he is now on the faculty

of the famous Massachusetts Institute of Technology (MIT).

will / may / should / ought to / might / could
Apparently, they believe that a reformed hacker ~~must~~ be

able to stop future cyber crimes. In short, while computer

hackers sometimes go to prison for their crimes, these days

be
their career opportunities may‸increasing.

6 Grammar for Writing
Using Modals to Hedge

Pre-writing Task

1 page 118

Possible answers:
It is about cyber crime. The writer believes they may be the hardest criminals to catch.

2 page 118

Cyber crime is a serious problem throughout the world for many reasons. Cyber criminals are extremely difficult to find. They (may) be the hardest criminals to catch. Cyber criminals (can) commit their crimes from anywhere in the world. Also, it (can) be impossible to know if they are working alone or with other cyber criminals. They do not need to be in the same place. Also, cyber criminals (may) be more educated and know more about computers than most other criminals. They (may) know more about the Internet than the police or even many computer specialists. Furthermore, no one knows how many cyber crimes have been committed. Some victims of cyber crimes (may) not have reported the crimes because they did not realize that a cyber crime happened to them. Another problem is that the laws against cyber crimes are changing all the time. In addition, some countries (may) not even have any clear laws against cyber crime yet. In the future, people will make more and more purchases and do more and more business using e-mail and the Internet. This (could) become riskier as cyber criminals continue to get smarter and harder to catch.

Writing Task

1 Write page 119

Answers will vary.

2 Self-Edit page 119

Answers will vary.

9 Nouns and Modifying Nouns
Attitudes Toward Nutrition

1 Grammar in the Real World

A page 120

Answers will vary; Possible answer: People are not as healthy today as they were in the past.

B Comprehension Check page 121

Possible answers:
1. They contain a great deal of fat and refined sugar but little or no nutrition.
2. They stayed active because work depended mostly on farming and physical labor.
3. Some diseases related to obesity are diabetes and heart disease.

C Notice page 121

1. NC; green and brown **food**
2. NC; (heart) **disease**
3. C; (food) **products**
4. NC; (the) **elderly**
5. NC; **obesity**

Part of speech: nouns and articles

2 Nouns
Exercise 2.1 Count Nouns

A page 123

2. are	8. are
3. suggest	9. has
4. is	10. have
5. suggest	11. contain
6. contain	12. enhance
7. has	

B Over to You page 124

Answers will vary.

Exercise 2.2 *The* + Adjective page 124

2. The poor	6. the disabled
3. the homeless	7. The unemployed
4. The elderly	8. the educated
5. The young	

Exercise 2.3 Count or Noncount Noun?

A page 125

2. s	11. X
3. X	12. X
4. s	13. X
5. X	14. X
6. X	15. s
7. es	16. X
8. X	17. s
9. X	18. X
10. X	

B Pair Work page 125

3. advice; abstract concepts
5. construction; areas of work
6. exercise; activities and sports
8. heart disease; diseases and health conditions
9. swimming; activities and sports
10. oxygen; elements and gases
11. dancing; activities and sports
12. gardening; activities and sports
13. research; abstract concepts
14. salt; particles
16. rice; food
18. information; abstract concepts

3 Noncount Nouns as Count Nouns

Exercise 3.1 Noncount Nouns with Count Meanings

A page 127

2. cheeses	11. fruits
3. coffees	12. coffee
4. teas	13. tea
5. cheese	14. sugar
6. cheeses	15. flour
7. experiences	16. sugars
8. time	17. flour
9. times	18. flours
10. fruit	

B Pair Work page 128

Answers will vary.

Exercise 3.2 Measurement Words with Noncount Nouns page 128

2. a game of
3. slice of / piece of / serving of
4. A serving of
5. A cup of / A glass of / A serving of
6. glasses of / servings of

7. a pinch of / a bit of
8. a grain of / a bit of / a piece of
9. drop of / bit of
10. a piece / a serving / a slice
11. a can of / a cup of / a serving of
12. a gallon of

Exercise 3.3 More Measurement Words with Noncount Nouns

A page 129

2. a wedge of cheese	5. two pieces of fish
3. two loaves of bread	6. one box of pasta
4. one bottle of water	

B Pair Work page 129

Answers will vary.

4 Modifying Nouns

Exercise 4.1 Order of Adjectives page 131

2. easy new Asian
3. useful government
4. small purple
5. new Thai; lovely rectangular; beautiful red
6. lovely white; tall antique glass

Exercise 4.2 More Order of Adjectives

A page 131

Answers will vary.

B Over to You page 132

Answers will vary.

Exercise 4.3 More Order of Adjectives

A page 132

2. delicious small	9. cotton and silk
3. fresh, delicious	10. tall white
4. spicy vegetarian	11. silver and gold
5. lovely, warm	12. rare, expensive
6. large, traditional	13. beautiful green and gold
7. fresh, crisp	14. delicious and memorable
8. beautiful, cozy	

B page 132

Same as **A**.

C Over to You page 132

Answers will vary.

5 Avoid Common Mistakes

Editing Task   page 133

ten-year-old
What does a ~~ten-years-old~~ child eat in a day? Specialists

are
in nutrition ~~is~~ finding out that the news is not good. As

a result, they are looking for ways to improve children's

habits
eating ~~habit~~. They are also involved in trying to help

choices
families make healthier ~~choice~~.

Most experts suggest that a few key practices can

is
help families. One of these practices ~~are~~ common sense:

people should eat unprocessed food. When there is a

choice between canned corn and fresh corn, people should

choose the fresh corn. Secondly, people should read labels

information
carefully. Because labels contain a lot of ~~informations~~,

people should familiarize themselves with the nutrition

and calorie content of their favorite products. Finally,

people can boost the health content of certain kinds of

flour
foods. For example, it is possible to substitute whole-grain ~~flours~~ for white flour in most recipes.

Parents and children live busy lives, but research shows

40-year-old
that when a healthy child becomes a ~~40-years-old~~ adult,

that person can look forward to a healthy old age.

6 Grammar for Writing
Using Precise Nouns and Adjectives to Make Your Writing Clearer

Pre-writing Task

1   page 134

Possible answers:
The writer suggests making small changes to increase exercise. The writer gives five suggestions.

2   page 135

Doctors say that most of their (overweight) patients know that they would benefit from some (lifestyle) changes. However, many of these (same) patients are quick to tell their doctors about their own (personal) reasons for not making these changes. (Overweight) children may prefer to play indoors rather than go outside and play. (Overweight) adults often say they are too busy at work.

Doctors and nutritionists have studied this problem. They have found that many (overweight) adults and children think they need to do a lot of (vigorous) exercise to get any benefit. This (false) belief discourages them, and so they end up doing nothing at all. (Recent) studies show that a little (light) exercise can help. Some suggestions for (small) changes include parking the car at the (far) end of a parking lot or getting off the bus one stop early. Another (practical) suggestion is taking stairs instead of elevators. Doctors also suggest that when watching TV, people walk or run in place during the commercials. Another (clever) idea for (working) adults and (busy) teens is to stand up and walk around when using the phone. (Big) changes can be scary and overwhelming, but (small) changes are not, so it is more likely that people will try them.
Precise nouns: doctors, patients, adults, nutritionists, children, teens

Writing Task

1 Write   page 135
Answers will vary.

2 Self-Edit   page 135
Answers will vary.

10 Articles and Quantifiers
Color

1 Grammar in the Real World

A   page 136
Answers will vary.

B Comprehension Check   page 137
Possible answers:
1. It is important to choose colors carefully because colors have a direct impact on feelings, so it is beneficial to choose colors that make people feel comfortable, happy, relaxed, or energized.
2. The decorator advised the Wangs to replace their icy blue carpet with one in warm colors and to replace their classic-style furniture with more comfortable pieces.
3. Yellow is cheerful and uplifting, green can revive the spirit, and blue is comforting.

C Notice   page 137

1. a   3. a
2. b   4. b

Use *a / an* when talking about an example, use *the* when talking about something in particular, and use no article when you're talking about something in general.

2 Indefinite Article, Definite Article, and No Article

Exercise 2.1 *A/An* or *The*? page 139

2. a	11. the
3. the	12. the
4. The	13. the
5. a/the	14. the
6. the	15. a
7. a	16. a
8. the	17. The
9. The	18. the
10. a/the	

Exercise 2.2 *A/An*, *The*, or No Article?

A page 140

2. ø	7. The
3. the	8. the
4. the	9. a
5. a	10. ø
6. a	11. the

B Over to You page 140

Answers will vary.

3 Quantifiers

Exercise 3.1 Quantifiers

A page 143

2. no	8. a little
3. Not many	9. none of
4. many	10. all
5. few	11. all
6. Quite a few	12. some
7. a little	

B Pair Work page 144

Answers will vary.

Exercise 3.2 More Quantifiers

A page 144

2. no	6. a great deal of / many of
3. many	7. few
4. Many of / a great deal of	8. quite a few
5. Most	

B pages 144–145

Answers will vary.

C Over to You page 145

Answers will vary.

Exercise 3.3 Using Quantifiers with *Of* page 145

3. X	8. X
4. of	9. of
5. X	10. of
6. of	11. X
7. of	

Exercise 3.4 More Quantifiers

A Over to You page 146

Answers will vary.

B Group Work page 146

Answers will vary.

4 Avoid Common Mistakes

Editing Task page 147

According to recent research, natural colors can help people remember things better. Felix A. Wichmann, *a* ^ research scientist, and two of his colleagues conducted experiments on color and memory. In the first experiment, participants looked at 48 photographs of nature scenes. None of the photographs were of people. Half of the photos were in black and white, and half were in color. Afterward, they looked at the same 48 photos mixed up with ~~alot~~ *a lot* of new photos. They had to say which ones they had already seen. They remembered the color scenes much better than the black-and-white ones. None of the participants were sure about all of the photos. Another experiment involved ~~much~~ *many* artificially colored photos. When artificially colored photos were included in the set of 48 photos, participants forgot ~~much~~ *many* of the photos. They did not remember the artificially colored photos any better than they remembered the black-and-white photos. These findings suggest that it is not just any colors that help to create ~~alot~~ *a lot* of our memories. Only natural colors have that power.

Why is this research important? For one thing, *an*~ advertiser may find these results interesting. If *an*~ advertiser uses natural colors in ads, consumers may be able to remember them better.

5 Grammar for Writing
Using Quantifiers and Pronouns to Hedge

Pre-writing Task

1 page 148

Answers will vary.

2 page 149

    <u>Many</u> people agree that colors can affect the way we feel. But most of the time, we may not be aware of the effect. Colors can even cause physical reactions. For example, a person might feel cold in a room with blue walls. If that same room were painted red, the same person might feel warm. Because of these physical reactions, <u>some</u> people believe that colors can heal. The use of colors to heal is called color therapy, or chromotherapy.

    Only <u>a few</u> people believe in chromotherapy. <u>Not many</u> traditional scientists believe in it. In fact, <u>quite a few of</u> them call it a "pseudoscience," which means that it is not based on any real, proven science. These scientists also argue that colors have different meanings in different cultures, so the same colors are unlikely to have the same effect on (all) patients. Furthermore, research has shown that the effects of a color are temporary. For example, people may feel happy while they are in a yellow room, but they will lose that feeling of happiness soon after they leave the room. The next time you feel warm or cold, happy or excited, look around you. Are colors affecting you?

Possible answer: The writer uses *all* because he or she is saying that not all people react the same way.

Writing Task

1 Write page 149

Answers will vary.

2 Self-Edit page 149

Answers will vary.

11 Pronouns
Unusual Work Environments

1 Grammar in the Real World

A page 150

Answers will vary; Possible answer: This workplace has a long list of perks and benefits.

B Comprehension Check page 151

Possible answers:
1. Some of the perks are free candy, on-site services, nature trails, and gourmet food in the cafeteria.
2. SAS gives its employees these perks to reduce distractions and encourage employees to interact with each other.
3. It shows that the perks and benefits are a success.

C Notice page 151

1. you
2. a benefit
3. the employees

2 Reflexive Pronouns
Exercise 2.1 Reflexive Pronouns

A page 153

2. itself	6. yourself
3. myself	7. himself
4. himself	8. yourselves
5. ourselves	

B Over to You page 153

Answers will vary.

Exercise 2.2 Reflexive Pronouns as Objects page 154

2. ourselves	6. me
3. myself	7. myself
4. herself	8. yourself
5. her	

Exercise 2.3 Other Uses of Reflexive Pronouns

A pages 154–155

2. herself	6 by themselves
3. myself	7. herself
4. by himself	8. themselves
5. himself	

B Group Work page 155

Answers will vary.

3 Pronouns with *Other / Another*

Exercise 3.1 *The Other, the Others, Others,* or *Another*?

A pages 156–157

2. others are
3. The other is
4. Another is
5. the others don't
6. Others include
7. Others are

B Over to You page 157

Answers will vary.

Exercise 3.2 *The Other, Another, Each Other,* or *One Another*? page 157

2. each other / one another
3. Another / The other
4. each other / one another
5. each other / one another
6. another
7. the other

4 Indefinite Pronouns

Exercise 4.1 Indefinite Pronouns page 159

2. everywhere
3. something
4. Everyone
5. everything
6. somebody
7. someone
8. something
9. anything
10. somewhere

Exercise 4.2 More Indefinite Pronouns

A page 160

2. anything
3. No one
4. anyone
5. No one
6. no one
7. anything
8. anywhere
9. nothing
10. nowhere

B page 160

1. 25–30 days; 6–14 days; 7–14 days; 10 days; 11 days
2. the European Union
3. the United States

C Pair Work page 160

Answers will vary.

5 Avoid Common Mistakes

Editing Task page 161

Management styles can vary widely. At one end of the extreme are the authoritarian managers who make all the decisions and are very strict. At the opposite end, there are ~~other~~ *others* who permit their employees to solve problems and suggest ideas ~~theirselves~~ *themselves*. Permissive managers are most effective when innovation and problem solving are part of the work process, for example, in technology. Stricter ones are effective when people are inexperienced or need a lot of guidance, or where there is high turnover of staff.

Mr. Jones is an example of an authoritarian manager. He relies only on ~~hisself~~ *himself* to make decisions at the restaurant where he works. Everyone ~~are~~ *is* expected to follow his orders exactly. His style works because employees are constantly changing, so nobody ~~need~~ *needs* to understand the rules and regulations.

Ms. Taylor is more democratic. The agents at her real estate agency manage their client accounts ~~theirselves~~ *themselves*. Some of her agents focus on business while ~~other~~ *others* work with private real estate accounts. It would be impossible for her to know what each agent is doing at any given time, so Ms. Taylor's style works well for her company.

There are different kinds of management styles ranging from very controlling to very open. Effective managers have a style of managing that is appropriate to the needs of their companies.

6 Grammar for Writing
Using Pronouns for Emphasis and
to Avoid Repetition

Pre-writing Task

1 page 162

Possible answer:
Team members must be able to communicate easily with
one another, be able to listen to each other, and be flexible
enough to compromise when they don't agree with one
another.

2 page 163

Job satisfaction means different things to different
people. However, for many people, the most important
thing is having good co-workers. For some people,
working with employees they like and respect is crucial.
These people feel the workday is much more pleasant when
they enjoy the people around them. For others, having
co-workers they like and respect isn't enough. They want
to be able to actually work cooperatively with other people.
These people generally like to work with people who are
good team players. Teams that work well follow important
rules. One is that members must be able to communicate
easily with (one another). Another is that team members
should be able to listen to (each other). Finally,
team members should be flexible enough to compromise
when they don't agree with (one another).

On the other hand, there are people who work better
alone. They don't want to have to deal with others all
the time. They say it slows them down to have to explain
themselves. They like to work with others who enjoy
working alone, but who are supportive and friendly and like
to talk once in a while. Whatever their preferred work style,
most people prefer working with people they like.

The reflexive pronoun *themselves* is an object of the
sentence with the same subject.

Writing Task

1 Write page 163

Answers will vary.

2 Self-Edit page 163

Answers will vary.

12 Gerunds
Getting an Education

1 Grammar in the Real World

A page 164

Answers will vary; Possible answer: Some ways to make
college more affordable are not attending a four-year
college right away or applying for financial aid.

B Comprehension Check page 165

Possible answers:
1. Public colleges depend on the government to help pay
   some of the expenses.
2. You do not have to repay a grant, but you must repay a
   loan with interest.
3. They can attend a community college for two years
   before transferring to a four-year college or apply for
   financial aid.

C Notice page 165

1. paying
2. repaying
3. Playing
The missing words are all gerunds (they end in *-ing*).
Subject: 3
Object: 1, 2

2 Gerunds as Subjects and Objects
Exercise 2.1 Gerunds as Subjects
and Objects

A pages 166–167

2. Finding the money for college is a problem for me.
3. My counselor suggests borrowing money for college.
4. Not getting into a good college worries me.
5. I enjoy discussing my future plans with my friends.
6. Not having enough money for tuition is a concern.
7. Going to interviews at schools makes me nervous.
8. Teachers suggest starting the application process early.

B Pair Work page 167

Subjects: 1, 2, 4, 6, 7
Objects: 3, 5, 8

Exercise 2.2 Gerunds as Objects

A page 167

2. keep studying
3. dislike writing
4. don't/do not delay thinking about
5. practice interviewing
6. consider paying
7. don't/do not mind borrowing
8. Discuss working
9. imagine working

B Group Work page 168

Answers will vary.

Exercise 2.3 More Gerunds as Objects

page 168

2. Bo is thinking about applying for financial aid instead of working.
3. Jane is avoiding borrowing money by getting a part-time job at school.
4. My parents and I aren't/are not discussing getting a loan.
5. Tom isn't/is not enjoying working while he goes to college.
6. My friend is delaying going back to school until he saves more money.
7. Lisa and Henry are discussing taking part in a work study program.
8. Mei-ling isn't/is not considering starting college without a part-time job.
9. Naresh is avoiding applying to too many different institutions.

3 Gerunds After Prepositions and Fixed Expressions

Exercise 3.1 Gerunds as Objects of Prepositions page 170

2. d	5. g
3. a	6. e
4. f	7. b

Exercise 3.2 More Gerunds as Objects of Prepositions

A pages 170–171

2. about paying	8. on talking
3. about taking	9. on majoring
4. about owing	10. in trying
5. about applying	11. about getting
6. for paying	12. about becoming
7. in asking	13. on teaching

B page 171

2. be afraid of applying for
3. be worried about paying
4. be interested in studying
5. be successful at teaching
6. concentrate on improving
7. depend on receiving

Exercise 3.3 Gerunds with Common Fixed Expressions

A page 172

2. reason for not doing
3. spend; time studying
4. have trouble keeping up
5. waste time partying
6. an interest in getting
7. in favor of giving
8. have difficulty affording

B page 172

*Same as **A**.*

C Group Work page 173

Answers will vary.

4 Gerunds After Nouns + *of*

Exercise 4.1 Nouns + *of* + Gerunds

A page 174

2. the fear of not being able to
3. the possibility of getting
4. the advantages of going
5. The benefits of attending
6. a possibility of getting
7. The process of applying
8. the risk of leaving

B Over to You page 174

Answers will vary.

5 Avoid Common Mistakes

Editing Task page 175

All students start the semester with the intention of
    studying   *finding*
~~study~~ hard; however, ~~find~~ time to study can be challenging.
            is
Finding good places to study ~~are~~ one challenge. Another is

finding enough hours in the day and creating a schedule.

Successful students face these problems realistically.

Different people have different purposes and needs when it comes to doing college work. ~~Study~~ *Studying* in a quiet library works well for some people. At the same time, a coffee shop or cafeteria can also be a good place to work for those who get energy from ~~be~~ *being* in a stimulating environment.

Then there is the question of time. Most students today are working, paying bills, and taking classes at the same time, so they do not have the luxury of ~~spend~~ *spending* many hours with their books. However, research offers hope. Studying for a few minutes several times a day ~~are~~ *is* a good way to learn new material.

~~Learn~~ *Learning* what works for you is the key to academic success.

6 Grammar for Writing
Using Noun + *of* + Gerund Constructions

Pre-writing Task

1 page 176

Possible answers:
The paragraph is about community college students. There are two advantages and three disadvantages listed.

2 page 177

Many students at community colleges do not go to school full-time because the <u>cost of getting</u> *subject* a degree requires them to work while they are in school. There are both <u>advantages and disadvantages of getting</u> *object* a degree while working. The disadvantages may be more obvious. First, students have to balance work, class, and homework. This can be particularly difficult to do sometimes. Also, students can face the <u>danger of losing</u> *object* interest. It can be hard to maintain interest in something that takes a very long time to complete. Another potential problem is that some classes are only offered at specific times. Students may not be able to change their work schedules to fit these classes into their schedules.

However, there are some advantages, too. Working students can usually finish their studies without having any loans to pay back. Some employers might also help their employees with their educational fees. In addition, working students sometimes have the <u>possibility of using</u> *object* what they learn in class at work. The <u>experience of working and going</u> *subject* to school at the same time can be difficult, but there are some important <u>advantages of being</u> *object* a part-time working student, too.

Writing Task

1 Write page 177
Answers will vary.

2 Self-Edit page 177
Answers will vary.

13 Infinitives
Innovative Marketing Techniques

1 Grammar in the Real World

A page 178

Answers will vary; Possible answer: A guerilla marketing campaign is successful if people talk about the ads.

B Comprehension Check page 179
Possible answers:
1. Guerrilla marketing is extreme advertising that uses surprising ways to advertise a good product and gets people's attention. Its purpose is to get people to talk about the ads.
2. It gets people's attention by using the environment in unexpected ways.
3. It is different from traditional advertising because it isn't afraid to shock people.

C Notice page 179
1. to do   2. to find   3. to use
The verbs are all infinitives. The words that appear before the infinitives are all verbs.

2 Infinitives with Verbs
Exercise 2.1 Verbs + Infinitives pages 180–181
2. hope to shock   5. seems to be
3. tends to cost   6. hesitate to admit
4. manages to generate

Exercise 2.2 Verbs + Objects + Infinitives

A page 181

2. gets consumers to notice
3. tell us not to do
4. convince them to try
5. persuade them to do
6. tell Mike to create
7. warn him to prepare

B Over to You page 182

Answers will vary.

Exercise 2.3 Verbs + Infinitives and Verbs + Objects + Infinitives page 182

2. chose to interview
3. urged me to interview
4. help to inform
5. help them to use
6. wants consumers to find out
7. promises to become
8. prepared to visit
9. encouraged me to contact
10. don't/do not need to offer
11. expect to include
12. would like to use

3 Infinitives vs. Gerunds

Exercise 3.1 Meanings of Infinitives vs. Gerunds

A page 184

2. LP Social Friends regrets telling the media that they pay people to be "friends."; D
3. I stopped reading the article about social media marketing.; D
4. Alison forgot to mention GamerWorld in her blog yesterday.; D
5. Upside Energy Drinks continues paying fans on social networking sites.; S
6. People have started to question Upside Energy Drinks' marketing strategy.; S
7. A lot of people can't stand to read blogs that are full of ads.; S
8. GamerWorld tried paying me to write about them in my blog.; D
9. I tried to change the privacy settings since I don't want messages from advertisers.; D

B Pair Work page 184

The meaning changes in 2, 3, 4, 8, and 9.

Exercise 3.2 Infinitive or Gerund?

A page 185

2. g
3. h
4. f
5. b
6. d
7. a
8. c

B page 185

Same as **A.**

4 Infinitives After Adjectives and Nouns

Exercise 4.1 *It* + *Be* + Adjective + Infinitive page 186

2. shocked to find out
3. easy to acquire
4. difficult to avoid
5. necessary to use
6. fun to go
7. interesting to read
8. unlikely to change

Exercise 4.2 Nouns + Infinitives page 187

2. It's/It is time to do something different now.
3. We made the decision to use QR codes yesterday.
4. We have the ability to attract the 18- to 24-year-old demographic.
5. It is a chance to introduce our products to athletes.
6. It's not / It isn't / It is not the best way to get messages across to older demographics.
7. It's/It is a chance to sell the product to viewers.

Exercise 4.3 Using Infinitives After Adjectives and Nouns

Group Work page 187

Answers will vary.

5 Avoid Common Mistakes

Editing Task page 188

Product placement in movies is a type of advertising that is popular today. Advertisers want ~~that~~ consumers ^to^ see their products in movies so that their products will seem more appealing. That's why advertisers pay filmmakers ~~for~~ ^to^ place their products in movies. For example, in one movie, a director arranged to ~~using~~ ^use^ a pair of famous brand-name sunglasses ~~for~~ ^to^ make his characters appear fashionable. In another movie, the plot required a

certain type of luxury car. The filmmakers used the car in

their film, but in this case they did not receive any money

from the auto's manufacturers. For the automaker, it

was an easy way~to~ ~not~ *not* pay for advertising. Filmmakers

seem~to~ ~not~ *not* mind the advertising because they can earn

extra money. Moviegoers do not seem to mind it, either.

   In my opinion, product placement in movies is

acceptable, but I want ~that~ advertisers~use~ *to* product

placement carefully. If directors expect to ~making~ *make* a

film that is believable, then everything in the film must

fit the story. Otherwise, the movie will seem more like

an advertisement. This would be terrible. I hope that

filmmakers continue to ~making~ *make* wise decisions and use

products that look natural on screen.

6 Grammar for Writing
Using Verb + Infinitive and Adjective +
Infinitive Constructions

Pre-writing Task

1 page 189

Possible answers:
The techniques are not creative. Companies continue to
use them because they are effective for certain products
and in certain environments.

2 page 189

   There are many new kinds of advertising techniques,
such as guerrilla advertising and reverse graffiti, but
it is (wrong to think) that the old techniques are gone.
Advertising companies continue to use many of them. For
example, ads have appeared inside buses and subways for
a long time. They are effective because they give people
on buses and subways (something to look at), and the
ads are inexpensive. Creativity with these ads is not
(necessary to grab) the audience's attention. These
techniques appear to be effective for certain products and
in certain environments. However, if a company wants its
(ads to be) very creative, these techniques are (unlikely to be)
the answer.
continue to use can also be written as *continue using*

44   Answer Key

Writing Task

1 Write page 189

Answers will vary.

2 Self-Edit page 189

Answers will vary.

14 Negative Questions and Tag Questions
Geographic Mobility

1 Grammar in the Real World

A page 190

Answers will vary; Possible answers: People move for jobs,
for better housing, and for family reasons.

B Comprehension Check page 191

Possible answers:
1. People move long distances for jobs and for family
   reasons.
2. People stay nearby when they move for better housing
   and for family reasons.
3. The mobility rate in Russia is lower than in the United
   States because available, affordable housing would take
   people further from family.

C Notice page 191

1. haven't
2. is

If the verb in bold is negative, then the verb you wrote is
affirmative. If the verb in bold is affirmative, then the verb
you wrote is negative.

2 Negative Questions
Exercise 2.1 Negative Questions page 193

2. Haven't you been listening
3. Can't you stop
4. Shouldn't you have bought
5. Aren't I
6. Weren't you going to take

Exercise 2.2 More Negative Questions
page 193

2. Haven't good schools made rich countries more
   attractive, too?
3. Don't some people move great distances to reunite with
   family members?
5. Isn't this happening more because of globalization?
6. Aren't the laws changing to allow even more movement?

Exercise 2.3 Responding to Negative Questions

Pair Work page 194

Answers will vary.

3 Tag Questions

Exercise 3.1 Tag Questions page 196

2. b   6. h
3. f   7. e
4. g   8. c
5. a

Exercise 3.2 Tags page 196

2. People can sometimes deduct moving costs from their income taxes, *can't they*?
3. Things have sometimes disappeared from a moving truck, *haven't they*?
4. Your friends will give you boxes, *won't they*?
5. Everyone should read reviews of a moving company before hiring one, *shouldn't they*?
6. Marta has been disorganized since the move, *hasn't she*?
7. Vinh and Ahn weren't moving today, *were they*?
8. It's been a stressful time for you, *hasn't it*?

Exercise 3.3 Statements in Tag Questions pages 196–197

2. Raul has relocated to London
3. Annette attended school in France
4. Miriam and Amir will turn down the promotion in New York
5. You didn't/did not like the air quality in Hong Kong
6. Bernard won't take the children with him to Texas

Exercise 3.4 Answering Tag Questions

page 197

2. No, they're not / they aren't / they are not
3. Yes, I have
4. No, I don't/do not
5. Yes, we will
6. No, I won't/will not
7. Yes, there are
8. Yes, it is

Exercise 3.5 Pronunciation Focus: Intonation and Meaning in Tag Questions

A page 198

No answers.

B page 198

2. But that college doesn't offer the major you want, does it?; U
3. Your son is thinking of going to college far from home, isn't he?; E
4. Duquesne University is in Pittsburgh, isn't it?; U
5. You're excited about moving to Pennsylvania for college, aren't you?; E
6. You're not worried about moving so far from home, are you?; U
7. Your son is worried about moving so far from home, isn't he?; E
8. But you and your wife feel OK about him moving so far away, don't you?; E

C Pair Work page 198

Answers will vary.

4 Avoid Common Mistakes

Editing Task page 199

A: That article on economic mobility in America was really
interesting, ~~no~~? *wasn't it*

B: It sure was. Some of the facts were surprising, ~~isn't it~~? *weren't they*

I was especially surprised that there is more economic

mobility in countries like France and Germany.

A: I was, too. I thought there was more mobility here. By

the way, don't you have a class right now?

B: ~~Yes~~. I'm finished for today. I'm free for the evening. *No*

A: But you're working tonight, ~~no~~? *aren't you*

B: No, I quit my job.

A: Really? Why? ~~You no~~ like it? *Don't/Didn't you*

B: The job was fine. The truth is I'm moving to Florida with

my family at the end of the semester, so I'm really busy.

A: You're kidding! Why? ~~Your family no~~ like it here? *Doesn't your family*

B: They like it here, but there aren't many good jobs. We're

moving where the jobs are.

A: But you only have one semester left, ~~isn't it~~? *don't you*

B: That's right, but I have to go with them.

5 Grammar for Writing
Using Negative Questions and Tag Questions in Blogs

Pre-writing Task

1 page 200

Possible answers:
"Boomerang kids" are students who move back in with their parents after college. Some reasons students move back home are because of the bad job market, to be closer to their parents, or because of the economy.

2 page 201

Damien: So, we've all agreed to focus the project on students moving back in with their parents after college, haven't we? The textbook said that there are more of these "boomerang kids" than before. Jo said she thought it was because of the bad job market. I agree that is one reason, but shouldn't there be other reasons, too? I think young people might be closer to their parents than they used to be. Wouldn't you guys agree?

Jo: I agree that many young people seem closer to their parents, but I don't know if that is a reason to move back home with them. Gabriel, you said that you think family is generally more important to people these days, didn't you?

Gabriel: Yes, I did. I'll try to find some articles. Don't you think that the economy has something to do with it? Young people feel insecure about their future. We could write about positive and negative reasons why young people live at home after college, couldn't we? What do you think?

The tag questions are used to confirm previous information. The negative questions are used to suggest new information.

Writing Task

1 Write page 201

Answers will vary.

2 Self-Edit page 201

Answers will vary.

15 *That* Clauses
Cultural Values

1 Grammar in the Real World

A page 202

Answers will vary.

B Comprehension Check page 203

1. b   2. a   3. c

C Notice page 203

1. believe that
2. have learned that
3. agree that
Number of subjects: two
Connecting word: that

2 *That* Clauses

Exercise 2.1 Forming *That* Clauses page 205

2. In fact, recent research has found that hard work doesn't always lead to wealth.
3. Many older Americans are realizing that they are unable to retire after working hard all their lives.
4. Many employees assumed that their companies would reward them for their hard work.
5. Researchers recently reported that job satisfaction has declined in recent years.
6. Employers are beginning to understand that it is important to give people some freedom at work.

Exercise 2.2 Using *That* Clauses Without *That*

Over to You page 205

Answers will vary.

Exercise 2.3 Using *That Clauses*

A page 206

2. Michael read that the average European gets about two months' vacation every year.
3. International labor statistics show that the average American works 46 weeks per year.
4. Some experts believe that culture may be one reason for the difference in attitudes toward work.
5. A group of scholars found that Europeans tend to value leisure more highly than Americans.
6. Some scholars believe that Americans tend to value earning money more highly than Europeans.
7. A professor at Gradina University wrote that many Americans seem to use possessions as a measure of success.

B Group Work page 206

Answers will vary.

3 Agreement Between *That* Clauses and Main Clauses

Exercise 3.1 *That* Clauses in Sentences with Present Verbs in the Main Clause page 208

2. Research shows that contemporary Latin American cultures have roots in African, European, and indigenous cultures.
3. Sociologists believe that Latin American cultures influenced world culture as well as U.S. culture.
4. Many musicologists agree that modern U.S. music is derived in part from Latin American cultures.
5. Many language experts assert that Spanish speakers contributed a great many words to the English language.
6. Most sociologists agree that Latin American cultures will continue / are going to continue to influence U.S. culture.

Exercise 3.2 *That* Clauses in Sentences with Past Verbs in the Main Clause page 209

3. thought that	9. felt that
4. would be	10. was taking
5. knew that	11. pointed out that
6. would have	12. was leading to
7. were aware that	13. did not realize that
8. was having	14. were destroying

Exercise 3.3 Agreement Between *That* Clauses and Main Clauses

Group Work page 209

Answers will vary.

4 *That* Clauses After Adjectives and Nouns

Exercise 4.1 *That* Clauses After Adjectives pages 211–212

2. Some people are worried that Americanization is making everything the same.
3. They are aware that Hollywood and fast-food chains are influencing culture.
4. I am convinced that culture is a two-way street.
5. I am positive that other cultures influence U.S. culture as much as U.S. culture influences them.
6. A lot of people are surprised that the French invented movies.

7. They are surprised that the British invented one of the original fast foods, fish and chips.
8. I am sure that we all benefit from global cultural exchange.

Exercise 4.2 *That* Clauses After Nouns and Adjectives

A Group Work page 212

Answers will vary.

B Over to You page 212

Answers will vary.

5 Avoid Common Mistakes

Editing Task page 213

Settlers from the east who traveled across the American West in the mid-nineteenth century understood ^*that* they faced a difficult journey across deserts and mountains. They knew/that the trip would take years and that some people ^*would* lose their lives. However, they were optimistic.

Michael T. Simmons was one of those determined travelers. Someone told him to go to the Pacific Northwest for new opportunities. He sold his business to pay for the supplies that he and his family needed. He knew that the area was largely unknown. He also knew that ^*it* was dangerous. This did not stop him.

When Simmons and his group reached Oregon, he announced that ^*he* was going to continue north. The Hudson's Bay Trading Company heard the news, and they discouraged him. However, Simmons was certain/that the trip ^*was* going to be successful, and he did not listen. Instead, he continued north as planned. After he arrived, he helped to establish the first settlement in the territory that is now known as Washington State. Documents show that Simmons built the first mill using water from the Tumwater waterfall for power. For this, he is sometimes called the father of Washington industry.

6 Grammar for Writing
Using *That* Clauses to State Reasons, Conclusions, Research Results, Opinions, and Feelings

Pre-writing Task

1 pages 214–215

Possible answers:
Students had problems speaking in class and not knowing what to call their teachers. The writer's information came from a study.

2 page 215

The first semester at college can be very difficult for international students. A recent study investigated the main difficulties international students had in their first semester in colleges in the United States and Canada. Ten students participated. The first difficulty <u>that students</u> <u>had was speaking in class</u>. There were a few reasons for this. One reason was <u>that the students were embarrassed</u> <u>about their English</u>. They felt <u>that it was not good enough</u>. However, <u>(it was unlikely that)</u> their English was not good. After all, each student had to receive a high score on an entrance exam in English. <u>(It is possible that)</u> the students <u>did not have enough confidence at first</u>. Many of the students were not used to speaking in class because they did not speak in class in their home countries. Another problem many students had was <u>that they did not know</u> <u>what to call their teachers</u>. The reason for this is <u>that</u> <u>the students call their teachers "Teacher" as a sign of</u> <u>respect when they are in their home countries</u>. However, they discovered <u>that *Teacher* sounded rude to some U.S.</u> <u>teachers</u>. The teachers asked the students to call them by their first names, although they realized <u>that some</u> <u>students would be uncomfortable with this at first</u>. It was interesting <u>that many of the students reported having these</u> <u>problems in the beginning</u>. However, most found <u>that they</u> <u>were able to adjust fairly quickly</u>.

These expressions introduce the writer's opinions and feelings.

Writing Task

1 Write page 215

Answers will vary.

2 Self-Edit page 215

Answers will vary.

16 Noun Clauses with *Wh-* Words and *If / Whether*
Inventions They Said Would Never Work

1 Grammar in the Real World

A page 216

Answers will vary; Possible answer: They faced skepticism and strong public doubt.

B Comprehension Check page 217

Possible answers:
1. People doubted him because he announced he had invented the light bulb before he had a model.
2. He convinced them when he lit up an entire New York neighborhood in 1882.
3. They had little formal education, they had no financial support, and they did not publicize their research.

C Notice page 217
1. when he would complete it
2. whether they had financial support
3. if their airplane would fly or not
1. a
2. b

2 Noun Clauses with *Wh-* Words
Exercise 2.1 Noun Clauses with *Wh-* Words

A pages 218–219
2. what she invented
3. who she is
4. why she invented it
5. when she invented it
6. where she was living
7. what the cell phone looked like
8. what it was made of

B Pair Work page 219

Answers will vary.

Exercise 2.2 Reduced Noun Clauses with *Wh-* Words + Infinitives pages 219–220

2. Amy wonders where to find a good patent lawyer.
3. I don't know how to find a manufacturer for our product.
4. Binh is wondering who to ask for money for our invention.
5. I'll figure out who to contact for financial advice.
6. I wonder what to charge for our product.

3 Noun Clauses with *If / Whether*

Exercise 3.1 Forming Noun Clauses with *If / Whether* page 221

2. Many people don't know if/whether some robots think like humans.
3. Many people don't know if/whether we can invent a nonpolluting fuel.
4. We can't remember if/whether anyone has invented a self-cleaning house.
5. Many people don't know about whether hybrid cars are good for the environment.
6. Scientists haven't figured out if/whether there are other planets humans can live on.

Exercise 3.2 Using Clauses with *If / Whether*

A page 222

Possible answers:

2. I don't know if/whether it will take a long time to invent it.
3. I don't know if/whether I am smart enough to do it by myself.
4. I don't know if/whether people really want solar-powered cars.
5. I don't know if/whether a solar-powered car will work on cloudy days.
6. I don't know if/whether my car is going to be too expensive.

B page 222

Possible answers:

2. I can't decide whether or not to take out a loan from the bank.
3. I can't decide whether or not to patent my idea first.
4. I can't decide whether or not to see a lawyer.

4 Noun Clauses in Direct and Indirect Questions

Exercise 4.1 Direct and Indirect Questions page 224

2. what your most famous invention is
3. if/whether you can show us an example

4. if/whether you market your gloves
5. where you were born
6. if/whether you studied art in college
7. how you became an artist
8. what your self-regenerating car is
9. how it works
10. what your first invention was

Exercise 4.2 More Indirect Questions

A page 225

Answers will vary.

B Pair Work page 225

No answers.

5 Avoid Common Mistakes

Editing Task page 226

Many inventions make life more convenient, but the Internet is the most essential one today. The Internet is a part of daily life. Although some people worry about *whether* ~~wheather~~ this fact is harmful or not, many agree that they do not know what ~~would~~ they *would* do if they could not go online.

First of all, the Internet helps people communicate instantly with family and friends who are far away. In the past, people had to write a letter or pay for a long-distance call to find out how ~~were~~ they *were* doing. While they waited, they worried about whether their loved ones were all right. Now there are many ways to contact people and find out if they are well.

In addition, the Internet helps people find information. If we want to know what ~~is~~ the temperature *is* in Seoul today, we only have to type the question. Also, it is very easy to look for employment, research solutions to a problem, and even find out *whether* ~~wether~~ a movie is playing nearby. It is too early to tell ~~either~~ *whether* the Internet causes serious problems for society or not. To me, it seems extremely valuable because it connects me to people I care about and to information I need.

6 Grammar for Writing

Using Noun Clauses with *Wh-* Words
and *If / Whether*

Pre-writing Task

1 page 227

Possible answers:
It is about the discovery of penicillin. The discoverer did
not realize why the fungus killed the bacteria or how to
produce it rapidly.

2 page 227

Penicillin is effective against many serious bacterial
infections. Alexander Fleming, a Scottish scientist,
discovered penicillin in 1928. However, he did not
immediately understand what he had discovered. At the
time, he was observing substances that could destroy
bacteria. However, Fleming was not a very neat scientist.
He often left trays of bacteria around his lab. In August
1928, he went away for a vacation. When he returned, he
found that something strange had happened to one of
the trays. A fungus had grown on the bacteria and killed
them. At first, Fleming did not understand why this had
happened, but he later realized what he had discovered.
He realized that the fungus was powerful and could be
useful in curing bacterial infections, but he still had not
understood how important it was. He doubted whether
the fungus could be effective long enough to kill bacteria
inside a human body. The penicillin he grew in the first few
years was too slow in taking effect, so he stopped working
on it. After a few years, he returned to it. Fleming and
other scientists discovered ways to make the substance
work more rapidly, and it soon became the most effective
antibiotic in existence. This discovery has saved millions
of lives.

Writing Task

1 Write page 227

Answers will vary.

2 Self-Edit page 227

Answers will vary.

17 Direct Speech and Indirect Speech

Human Motivation

1 Grammar in the Real World

A page 228

Answers will vary; Possible answer: Internal rewards are
particularly effective in motivating workers.

B Comprehension Check page 229

	External Reward	Internal Reward
1.	✓	
2.		✓
3.		✓
4.	✓	
5.	✓	

C Notice page 229

1. said   2. told   3. informed
Actual words: 1
You know because quotation marks are used.

2 Direct Speech

Exercise 2.1 Statements in Direct Speech

A pages 230–231

Possible answers:
2. Mike Ditka said, "The ones who want to achieve and win
   championships motivate themselves."
3. Nolan Bushnell said, "The ultimate inspiration is the
   deadline."
4. Dwight D. Eisenhower said, "Motivation is the art of
   getting people to do what you want them to do because
   they want to do it."
5. Thomas Jefferson said, "I'm a great believer in luck, and I
   find the harder I work, the more I have of it."
6. Fernando Flores said, "Great work is done by people
   who are not afraid to be great."
7. Ralph Waldo Emerson said, "Nothing great was ever
   achieved without enthusiasm."
8. Wayne Gretzky said, "You miss 100 percent of the shots
   you don't take."
9. Lao Tzu said, "The journey of a thousand miles begins
   with a single step."

B Over to You page 231

Answers will vary.

C Pair Work page 231

Answers will vary.

Exercise 2.2 Questions in Direct Speech

A page 232

2. "Do you have guidelines for rewarding employees?" asked Pedro. *OR* "Do you have guidelines for rewarding employees?" Pedro asked.
3. Roxana asked, "When should you give the rewards?"
4. "What are some ways to motivate employees?" asked Hong. *OR* "What are some ways to motivate employees?" Hong asked.
5. Chelsea asked, "Can you give an example of what you mean?"

B Over to You page 232

Answers will vary.

3 Indirect Speech

Exercise 3.1 Tense Shifts in Indirect Speech page 234

2. A student said (that) the class was discussing motivation and personality this week.
3. The professor said (that) the class was reading about Abraham H. Maslow's theories on motivation.
4. One student said (that) he/she was learning a lot in the class.
5. Another student said (that) he/she didn't understand the lectures.
6. The teaching assistant said (that) the readings have great practical value.

Exercise 3.2 Modals and Future Forms in Indirect Speech page 235

2. She said (that) the course would rely heavily on participants' own experiences.
3. She said (that) we might occasionally have guest speakers.
4. She said (that) the course would include presentations, homework, and weekly quizzes.
5. She said (that) there would be three papers and two oral presentations.
6. She said (that) participants could substitute an oral presentation for one of the papers.

4 Indirect Speech Without Tense Shift

Exercise 4.1 Keeping the Original Tense in Indirect Speech pages 236–237

Possible answers:
2. The manager said (that) the client loves it.
3. Janet said (that) we have always solved these problems in the past.
4. Janet said (that) staff satisfaction has been very important.

5. Rodrigo said (that) tomorrow we are going to have a half-day training session on giving constructive feedback.
6. Rodrigo said (that) we/they will all work together, as a team.

Exercise 4.2 Using Present Tense Reporting Verbs

A page 237

2. is
3. enjoys
4. enjoys
5. 's not / isn't / is not
6. should; ask

B Pair Work page 237

Answers will vary.

5 Other Reporting Verbs

Exercise 5.1 Other Reporting Verbs page 239

2. said
3. told
4. reminded
5. informed
6. explained
7. informed
8. remarked
9. admitted
10. reminded
11. remarked

Exercise 5.2 More Reporting Verbs

A pages 239–240

2. reminded us
3. suggested that
4. stated that
5. mentioned that
6. explained that
7. reported that
8. claimed that
9. informed us that
10. showed that
11. explained that

B page 240

*Same as **A**.*

C Over to You page 240

Answers will vary.

6 Avoid Common Mistakes

Editing Task page 241

One of the highlights of my life happened through an experience at work. It started when my manager announced ~~us~~ *to us* some interesting news. He said, "I am starting a company band." Then he asked, "Who wants to join?" I mentioned *to* him that I had played guitar for many years. He said, "You should definitely try out."

On the day of tryouts, I was a little nervous because everyone played extremely well. After I auditioned, the manager thanked me and explained ^to me that he ~~will~~ *would* let me know soon.

I forgot about it, so I was very surprised when I got a phone call from my manager a few days later. He said, "You can play lead guitar." I said, "Wow! That's great!" After that, the band practiced a few times a week. A few months later, we played at the company party. We were nervous, but we played well. The president of the company spoke to me later and said I ~~have~~ *had* a lot of talent. I was embarrassed by his compliment, but I said I ~~am~~ *was* proud to play for the company. I will never forget that experience.

7 Grammar for Writing
Using Descriptive Reporting Verbs

Pre-writing Task

1 page 242

Possible answers:
The survey took place in a gym. The purpose of the survey was to get advice on how the writer could motivate himself / herself. The writer decided to try all of the suggestions.

2 page 243

I find it hard to motivate myself to exercise, so I went to a gym to get some advice. I (asked) people what motivated them. A few of the people (said) that they made exercise a routine or habit. They (explained) that they didn't think about whether or not to go to the gym on any particular day. They just went on the same days every week. One of the trainers there (swore) that money was one of the most important motivators. She (argued) that people who paid for something tended to use it more.

Two other people (told) me that they promised themselves a reward each week that they went to the gym three times. They (claimed) that they wouldn't reward themselves if they missed a day. (I asked) them what their rewards usually were, and they (explained) that they often went out to dinner with friends as a reward. I (pointed out) that having dinner in a restaurant might ruin the benefits of going to the gym, but they (assured) me that they always ate healthy meals at restaurants. I decided I could use all of these ideas for motivation, so I joined the gym.

Writing Task

1 Write page 243
Answers will vary.

2 Self-Edit page 243
Answers will vary.

18 Indirect Questions; Indirect Imperatives, Requests, and Advice
Creative Problem Solving

1 Grammar in the Real World

A page 244
Answers will vary.

B Comprehension Check page 245
Possible answers:
1. The rules are not to judge other people's ideas, shout out even unusual ideas, produce a large number of ideas, and look for ways to improve on other ideas.
2. Michalko believes that brainwriting may be more productive than brainstorming because people think of additional ideas as they write, it is better for quieter individuals, and they don't have to express their ideas out loud.
3. According to the writer, anyone can use brainstorming.

C Notice page 245
1. not to judge
2. to shout out
They both use the infinitive.

2 Indirect Questions
Exercise 2.1 Forming Indirect Questions
pages 246–247

Possible answers:
2. Joanna asked Dr. Martin why creative thinking will be even more important in the future.
3. Joanna asked what techniques have worked to get people to think creatively.
4. Joanna asked how moving promotes creativity.
5. Joanna asked if there are any other ideas like this.
6. Joanna asked if objects and colors stimulate creative thinking.

Exercise 2.2 More Forming Indirect Questions pages 247–248

Possible answers:

2. He asked her if the session was here.
3. He asked her who her leader was.
4. He asked her what she did with the paper and the markers.
5. He asked her how long she was drawing pictures.
6. He asked her why she watched TV in the office.
7. He asked her if she is going to continue tomorrow.

Exercise 2.3 Using Indirect Questions

Group Work page 248

Answers will vary.

3 Indirect Imperatives, Requests, and Advice

Exercise 3.1 Indirect Imperatives and Requests page 249

2. Then she said not to get into a group with someone you usually work with.
3. She told us to cut out pictures from magazines that show our ideal working environment.
4. Dr. Martin said not to criticize our group members' choices.
5. Then she told us to present our picture to the other groups.
6. After that, she said to comment on the other groups' pictures, but not to criticize people's choices.
7. Finally, Dr. Martin said to discuss the emotions that the pictures suggest.

Exercise 3.2 Indirect Requests and Advice page 250

2. The husband asked to take a different pencil.
3. The wife asked to use her own pen.
4. The therapist said to write for 15 minutes without stopping.
5. The therapist told the clients not to look at each other's writing during the activity.
6. The therapist said not to talk to each other.
7. The therapist told the clients to be prepared to read their descriptions to each other.
8. The husband asked to have a little more time to write.

Exercise 3.3 Indirect Advice

A Over to You page 250

Answers will vary.

B Group Work page 251

Answers will vary.

4 Avoid Common Mistakes

Editing Task page 251

When my psychology professor asked our class ~~did~~ *if* we ~~want~~ *wanted* to try brainstorming as part of our next group project, I had no idea that the experience would be so challenging or successful. First, when we started, one of our members asked many unimportant questions. When the team leader asked her ~~that she asks~~ *to ask* the questions later, that person began complaining. Then the team leader asked the person ~~did~~ *if* she ~~want~~ *wanted* to be the group leader. The rest of us told *her/him* this was a bad idea, and there was an argument. A different problem arose when we met the second time. The leader asked one student ~~that he takes~~ *to take* electronic notes, but he forgot. As a result, when we met the third time, the leader had to tell *us* the information again. She asked me ~~that I~~ *to* write the notes this time, and I did. Aside from these minor problems, the group generated a lot of ideas and finally came up with a successful proposal for a project. So, if someone asked me ~~do~~ *if* I ~~want~~ *wanted* to work as a group again, I would say yes because even though it is hard to work as a group, the outcome can be better.

5 Grammar for Writing
Using Indirect Questions, Imperatives, Requests, and Advice

Pre-writing Task

1 pages 252–253

Possible answers:
The focus of their project is creative problem-solving strategies. There are four students in the group.

2 page 253

Clara: Professor Moss <u>asked us to write outlines for our</u> *Q* <u>reports on good problem-solving strategies</u>. He <u>said to</u>

A
identify our own creative problem-solving processes before we try to find new ones. I'll start. When I have a problem I can't solve, I think about my older sister, Susannah. She's really good at solving difficult problems. I ask myself how
Q
Susannah would solve the problem. That helps me to think about things in a different way.

Carmen: That's interesting, Clara. I never thought of doing that. I have a different technique. A few years ago, I
I
had a teacher who always told us to try to solve problems by thinking of the end result we wanted and working backward. I try to do that sometimes. Why don't we try everyone else's creative thinking processes and see how they work? Also, could everyone say when they can meet next?

Jun: I don't think I use any special creative problem-solving strategies.

Hao: Jun, Carmen asked if we could try each other's
Q
strategies. If you don't have one, why don't you just try everyone else's and let us know how they work for you?

Carmen: I just realized it's already Thursday and no one has written here for a while. We have to get working. Does anyone remember when we have to turn in our outline?
Q
Jun: Yes, I asked Prof. Moss when our outline was due.
Q
Prof. Moss asked if we could turn it in by Friday. He said he could get us some feedback by Monday. He told us not to
I
spend too much time on the outline, though, because he wants to approve our ideas before we write our report.

Writing Task

1 Write page 253

Answers will vary.

2 Self-Edit page 253

Answers will vary.

19 The Passive (1)
English as a Global Language

1 Grammar in the Real World

A page 254

Answers will vary; Possible answer: English is important to learn because it's becoming a global language.

B Comprehension Check page 255

Possible answers:
1. English is being spoken around the world.
2. People around the world speak English in their jobs, on the Internet, and when traveling.
3. Some disadvantages might include the loss of cultural identity and the creation of dialects.

C Notice page 255

1. b
2. c
3. a
The verbs in B have a form of *be* and are in the past participle form. The verbs in A are in the simple present.

2 Active vs. Passive Sentences
Exercise 2.1 Active and Passive Sentences

A page 258

2. speak	7. Does BR Corporation support
3. use	8. offers
4. isn't used	9. Are the courses taught
5. is needed	10. conduct
6. expect	

B Pair Work page 258

4. No, they don't use English much.
5. Executives who travel need English.
9. Do native English speakers teach the courses?

C Group Work page 258

2. Yes, English is spoken by most executives at this branch.; necessary
3. I mean, is English used here by lower level employees, too?; necessary
6. Executives are expected (by us) to read technical documents in English.; not necessary
7. Is English language learning supported by BR Corporation?; necessary
8. Yes, onsite English courses are offered (by BR Corporation).; not necessary
10. Yes, all of our English classes are conducted by native speakers.; necessary

Exercise 2.2 Present Forms of the Passive page 259

2. is; spoken
3. have been included
4. are offered
5. has been taught
6. is offered
7. has been reported
8. has been estimated / is estimated

Exercise 2.3 Past Forms of the Passive

A page 260

2. *The ancient Romans spoke Latin.*; Latin was spoken by the ancient Romans.
3. *Ancient Roman authors wrote many important manuscripts.*; Many important manuscripts were written by ancient Roman authors.
4. *For many centuries, the Romans conquered neighboring nations.*; For many centuries, neighboring nations were conquered by the Romans. *OR* Neighboring nations were conquered by the Romans for many centuries.
5. *These conquered groups spoke versions of Latin.*; Versions of Latin were spoken by these conquered groups.
6. *Conquered people from Britain to Africa used Latin.*; Latin was used by conquered people from Britain to Africa.
7. *People were still speaking Latin after the Roman Empire fell.*; Latin was still being spoken (by people) after the Roman Empire fell. *OR* After the Roman Empire fell, Latin was still being spoken (by people).
8. *Scholars and scientists were using Latin until the eighteenth century.*; Latin was being used by scholars and scientists until the eighteenth century. *OR* Until the eighteenth century, Latin was still being used by scholars and scientists.

B page 260

7. Latin was still being spoken after the Roman Empire fell. *OR* After the Roman Empire fell, Latin was still being spoken.

3 Verbs and Objects with the Passive

Exercise 3.1 Transitive or Intransitive?
pages 261–262

2. *People don't use Latin for everyday communication today.*; Latin isn't used for everyday communication today.
3. *Some languages die.*; X
4. *This occurred with Dalmatian.*; X
5. *People spoke Dalmatian in Croatia.*; Dalmatian was spoken in Croatia.
6. *Dalmatian speakers lived in coastal towns of Croatia.*; X

7. *Groups in different regions developed dialects of Dalmatian.*; Dialects of Dalmatian were developed.
8. *Native speakers didn't record the grammar of Dalmatian.*; The grammar of Dalmatian wasn't recorded.

Exercise 3.2 Using Transitive and Intransitive Verbs

A Over to You page 262

Answers will vary.

B Group Work page 262

No answers.

Exercise 3.3 Direct Objects in Passive Sentences

A–B page 262

1. (The first book about Esperanto) was published by a company in 1887.
2. (Esperanto) was invented by L. L. Zamenhof.
3. (Esperanto) was created by its inventors to be a very easy language to learn.
4. (The grammar) was designed by Zamenhof to be simple and clear.
5. (It) is spoken by about 10,000 people.
6. (It) is being used by people in about 115 countries.
7. (It) has not been recognized as an official language by any country.
8. (The language) is used by some international travelers.

4 Reasons for Using the Passive

Exercise 4.1 Describing Processes and Results

A pages 263–264

2. were given an essay-writing assignment
3. was taught essay-writing techniques only
4. were taught both essay-writing techniques and grammar
5. were read by a group of judges
6. were put into the folder
7. were rated from 1 to 5(, with 5 being the best)
8. were given ratings of 2 or 3
9. are included in the same course

B page 264

Same as **A.**

Exercise 4.2 Reporting News Events
pages 264–265

2. The importance of preserving the Native American languages was recognized.
3. Data on the use of the Ojibwe and Dakota languages was collected.
4. In Minnesota, the Ojibwe and Dakota languages were no longer spoken OR The Ojibwe and Dakota languages were no longer spoken in Minnesota.
5. A strategy was developed to teach the Ojibwe and Dakota languages in schools OR A strategy to teach the Ojibwe and Dakota languages in schools was developed.
6. Teacher-training programs are being developed.
7. In 2011, software for teaching the Ojibwe language was released OR Software for teaching the Ojibwe language was released in 2011.
8. Native Americans' cultural identities will be strengthened.

Exercise 4.3 Avoiding Blame and Criticism page 265

Possible answers:
2. Some material from the Internet was copied in the essay.
3. Last night, the school's e-mail system was broken into.
4. The paper was not edited carefully.

5 Avoid Common Mistakes
Editing Task page 266

Even good writers will tell you that English spelling has ~~been~~ confused them at one time or another. The same sound *is* ~~spelled~~ many different ways. For example, the words *lazy* and *busy* are ~~pronouncing~~ *pronounced* with a /z/ sound, but they are not consistent in their spelling because of strange rules that are ~~being~~ related to the vowels. Why *is* English ~~is~~ written this way? English is an ancient language that contains old spelling rules. Also, other languages have ~~been~~ contributed many words to English.

Some experts who ~~have been studied~~ *have studied / have been studying* the English language for years would like to see English spelling simplified. They ask important questions: Why *is* so much time ~~is~~ wasted on spelling lessons? Why is literacy lower in English-speaking countries than in countries with simplified spelling? They point to the fact that many other languages *were* ~~simplified~~

successfully. They suggest that in places such as Sweden, France, and Indonesia, changes to the written form have helped make learning to read easier.

6 Grammar for Writing
Using the Passive to Write About the Object of an Action

Pre-writing Task

1 pages 266–267

Possible answers:
American, British, and Jamaican English are being compared.

2 page 267

English is spoken in many countries around the world, but in most places, it is more similar to British English than it is to American English. However, Jamaican English is different. The English that is spoken in Jamaica has similarities to both British and American English. Because Jamaica was once a British colony, Jamaican English used to be similar to British English. However, because Jamaican people get more exposure to American media than to British media these days, and because Jamaica is so close to North America, many changes have occurred. For example, in Jamaica, people say *do you have* instead of the British *have you got*. In addition, *you don't need to do that* is used instead of the British expression *you needn't do that*. Also, many American English words are used in Jamaica in place of their British equivalents. For example, baby beds are *cribs* rather than the British *cots*, and people live in *apartments* rather than the British *flats*. Despite the changes in expressions and vocabulary, the words are pronounced in a more British way than in an American way. As English becomes more of a global language, it will be interesting to see what other changes occur.

The agent: Jamaicans / Jamaican English speakers
The agent is obvious.

Writing Task

1 Write page 267

Answers will vary.

2 Self-Edit page 267

Answers will vary.

20 The Passive (2)
Food Safety

1 Grammar in the Real World

A page 268

Answers will vary; Possible answer: Some genetically modified foods are sweet corn and soybeans.

B Comprehension Check page 269

Possible answers:
1. Genetically modified foods are foods which come from plants that have been changed in a laboratory.
2. Some advantages of genetically modified foods are that they can resist insects, resist powerful weed-killing chemicals, and produce more food in a shorter time.
3. Some concerns about genetically modified foods are that they haven't been tested adequately for safety, their use has caused weeds to no longer be affected by weed killer, and they won't solve world hunger because world hunger is due to unequal food distribution.

C Notice page 269

1. should be designed
2. will not be solved
3. should; be taken
The verb *be* comes after the modals in passive verb forms.

2 The Passive with *Be Going To* and Modals

Exercise 2.1 The Passive with *Will* and *Be Going To* pages 270–271

2. will be discussed
3. are going to be addressed
4. are going to be debated
5. are going to be promoted
6. be improved
7. will not be solved
8. will not be increased
9. will be presented
10. will be addressed
11. will be demonstrated

Exercise 2.2 The Passive with Modals

A page 271

Possible answers:
2. Air pollution can be caused by pesticides.
3. In the United States, pesticides can be found (by scientists) in many streams.
4. Some farm animals may have been harmed by pesticides.
5. Meat from farm animals may have been affected by pesticides.
6. Fish could be affected by pesticides in water.
7. In some cases, humans can be affected by pesticides.

B Pair Work page 271

Same as **A**.

Exercise 2.3 More Passive with Modals
page 272

2. The package must not be opened.
3. The product must not be consumed.
4. The product can be returned for a refund.
5. Questions about the product you bought may be asked (by store management).
6. A similar product might be offered to you (by store management).

Exercise 2.4 Using Passive Forms of Modals

Group Work page 273

Answers will vary.

3 *Get* Passives
Exercise 3.1 *Get* Passives pages 274–275

2. Our lettuce got contaminated
3. Did the lettuce get recalled by the FDA
4. it got recalled
5. our produce gets picked
6. It also gets packed
7. It sometimes gets mishandled
8. the workers got distracted
9. Doesn't your produce get checked
10. it doesn't get inspected

Exercise 3.2 More *Get* Passives

A Over to You page 275

Answers will vary.

B Group Work page 275

Answers will vary.

4 Passive Gerunds and Infinitives

Exercise 4.1 Passive Gerunds and Infinitives page 277

2. being
3. being
4. to be
5. to be
6. being

Exercise 4.2 More Passives Gerunds and Infinitives

A pages 277–278

2. to be sold
3. to be told
4. being; informed
5. being fooled
6. being poisoned
7. to be fooled
8. to be used
9. being confused

B Over to You page 278

Answers will vary.

C Pair Work page 278

No answers.

5 Avoid Common Mistakes

Editing Task page 279

It is certain that many advances in technology will be
made
~~make~~ in the twenty-first century. Although many of these

advances will improve our future, others may do as much

harm as good. GM foods are one example. Currently, many
being created
new foods are ~~creating~~ by scientists. For instance, many

people suffer from food allergies. Certain GM foods may
changed
help avoid this problem; the food's DNA has been ~~change~~

so that the food no longer causes allergic reactions. Also,
fed
one day, the world's growing population may be ~~feed~~ with

GM foods that grow quickly. This will make it possible for
produced   *used*
more food to be ~~produce~~. These new foods can be ~~use~~ to

feed more people. However, GM foods have another side.

Because these foods have not existed very long, scientists

do not know all their effects. For example, some people fear
be caused
that cancer can ~~cause~~ by GM foods. This is especially
be marked
troubling because GM foods might not ~~mark~~ as such, so

consumers may not know what they are buying. When

they develop new foods, scientists should be aware of the

concerns that consumers have. In my view, we should be

careful with any new technology.

6 Grammar for Writing

Using the Passive with Modals, Gerunds, and Infinitives

Pre-writing Task

1 page 280

Possible answers:
The reasons the writer gives are that some foods are
protected from pesticides by a thick peel and others are not
attractive to bugs.

2 page 280

Buying organic foods has been popular for a long time,
but it can be expensive. Some organic foods may not be
worth the extra expense. For example, consumers do not
necessarily have to buy organic bananas. The reason for
this is that the banana itself seems <u>to be protected</u> from
the pesticides by the thick banana peel. Other nonorganic
foods that have thick peels or skins and that <u>can be eaten</u>
safely are avocados and watermelons. There are also some
nonorganic foods that are safe for other reasons. For
example, some foods are simply not attractive to bugs, so
it is a waste of farmers' time and money to spray pesticides
on these foods. No one is sure why, but the reason for this
might be that insects don't like the taste of these foods.
Broccoli, cabbage, and onions fall into this category.
However, these nonorganic foods <u>can</u> still <u>be priced</u> higher
because no chemical residue <u>can be found</u> in them. <u>Should</u>
the public <u>be informed</u> of this? Consumers should be
worried about not (being made aware) of this information
since they <u>could be spending</u> more than they need to.

Writing Task

1 Write page 281

Answers will vary.

2 Self-Edit page 281

Answers will vary.

21 Subject Relative Clauses (Adjective Clauses with Subject Relative Pronouns)

Alternative Energy Sources

1 Grammar in the Real World

A page 282

Possible answers: Some alternative sources of energy are wind, sun, and water.; *Answers will vary.*

B Comprehension Check page 283

Possible answers:

1. Some ways that people can make energy are by using special exercise equipment which can convert human energy into electricity and by walking on special surfaces to generate energy.
2. "People power" helps the environment because it is a sustainable energy source, and it reduces carbon dioxide output.
3. Some problems with people power are that it doesn't produce a lot of energy and the development of the technology is moving slowly.

C Notice page 283

1. Professional athletes, <u>whose</u> **exercise routines** can last for several hours, could help power a house!

2. This heat, <u>which</u> **is sent** to a nearby building, cuts the energy bill by 25 percent.

3. However, people <u>who</u> **support** green energy are confident that this technology will catch on in the near future.

1. noun
2. verb
3. verb

2 Identifying Subject Relative Clauses

Exercise 2.1 Subject Relative Pronouns

A page 285

2. which connects	7. which saves
3. which keeps	8. which illustrates
4. which powers	9. which provides
5. which use	10. who take
6. who runs	

B page 285

Same as **A.**

Exercise 2.2 Definitions with Identifying Relative Clauses

A page 285

2. that doesn't/does not disappear
3. who/that study
4. who/that puts
5. who/that designs

B page 286

2. someone who/that works to protect the environment
3. people who/that are part of a political group focused on good environmental policy
4. chemicals which/that trap heat in the atmosphere
5. a vehicle which/that uses two sources of power to run
6. a type of energy which/that uses the sun as its source
7. a type of energy which/that comes from human exercise
8. structures which/that don't/do not have a large negative impact on the environment.

Exercise 2.3 Sentence Combining

A–B pages 286–287

2. GreenGo developed a technology <u>which/that turns exercise machines into power generators.</u>

3. GreenGo builds machines like exercise bikes <u>which/that let exercisers generate electricity from their workouts.</u>

4. The electricity connects to a power grid <u>which/that covers a large geographic area.</u>

5. Sachiko Hanley is the woman <u>who/that invented this technology.</u>

6. Many GreenGo clients are colleges and other institutions <u>which/that have on-site gyms.</u>

7. GreenGo provides an energy source <u>which/that is good for the environment.</u>

8. "We are proud to do work with institutions <u>which/that have the same environmental goals that we do.</u>"

3 Nonidentifying Subject Relative Clauses

Exercise 3.1 Identifying or Nonidentifying?

A pages 288–289

As the environment changes, hurricanes and other severe storms have become a serious problem in the United States and Latin America. Hurricanes, <u>which primarily</u> *NI* <u>attack southern and southeastern parts of the United States</u>, have been increasing in severity. The hurricane *I* <u>that did the most damage in recent history</u> was Hurricane Katrina. Since then, a great number of Americans, including many celebrities, have helped the people of New Orleans rebuild their homes.

The celebrity <u>who is best known for building homes in</u> *I* <u>New Orleans</u> is Brad Pitt. Pitt, <u>who created a foundation</u> *NI* <u>called Make It Right</u>, helps build new "green" homes in New Orleans. The goals of this foundation are admirable. *NI* Make It Right volunteers, <u>who work for free</u>, want to build 150 new green homes in the Lower 9th Ward.

The foundation is not simply providing new homes. Make It Right homes have many features <u>which are</u> *I* <u>environmentally sound</u>. For example, Make It Right homes have metal roofs <u>which absorb heat and keep them cool</u>. *I* It is possible that Make It Right homes will inspire new home builders not only in New Orleans but around the world as well.

B Pair Work page 289

Answers will vary.

Exercise 3.2 Nonidentifying Subject Relative Clauses pages 289–290

2. The Turning Torso building, which is located in Malmö, Sweden, uses only renewable energy.
3. The Turning Torso building, which is the tallest building in Sweden, was inspired by a sculpture of a twisting human being.

4. The Burj al-Taqa, which will be in Dubai, will be a wind- and solar-powered green skyscraper.
5. Eckhard Gerber, who designed the Burj al-Taqa, has also designed a green building in Riyadh.
6. Architect Eric Corey Freed, who has written several books on building green structures, believes that people will pay more for green buildings.

4 Subject Relative Clauses with *Whose*

Exercise 4.1 Subject Relative Clauses with *Whose*: Identifying or Nonidentifying?

A page 291

Meet Charles Greenwood, the inventor of a new type of car. Greenwood, <u>whose human-powered car can go up to 60 miles per hour</u>, is an engineer. This inventor, <u>whose dream is to sell the cars to the public</u>, has also started a business to manufacture it. A car <u>whose power source is human energy</u> is obviously good for the environment. How does it work? The car, <u>whose main power source is human-operated hand cranks</u>, also runs with a battery. It's not expensive, either. The car – the HumanCar Imagine PS – sells for about $15,000. A hybrid car <u>whose selling price will only be about $15,000</u> should be very popular with energy-conscious consumers.

There are other benefits to a human-powered car. A car <u>whose power source is human energy</u> might also help drivers stay fit. In addition, owners expect to save money operating the HumanCar. The HumanCar, <u>whose main source of power is human-operated hand cranks</u>, gets the equivalent of 100 miles to the gallon of gas in a regular car.

B Pair Work page 291

lines 1–2: nonidentifying
lines 2–3: nonidentifying
line 4: identifying
line 5: nonidentifying
line 7: identifying
lines 9–10: identifying
lines 12–13: nonidentifying

Exercise 4.2 *That, Who,* or *Whose?* page 292

2. whose	7. that
3. that	8. whose
4. that	9. that
5. whose	10. who/that
6. whose	

Exercise 4.3 Subject Relative Clauses with *Whose*

Pair Work page 292

Answers will vary.

5 Avoid Common Mistakes

Editing Task page 293

People think renewable energy only comes from water, wind, or the sun, but there is another renewable energy source: biofuels. Biofuels are fuels ~~who~~ *which/that* are derived from oils in plants. Farmers ~~who's~~ *whose* fields were once planted with food crops can now grow energy on their land. The most commonly used example of this is ethanol, a biofuel ~~who~~ *which/that* is usually made from corn and added to gasoline. However, ethanol has been criticized. Some critics say that the world, ~~who's~~ *whose* population continues to grow, needs all of its corn for food production. Others have argued that it takes too much energy to produce corn ethanol. Recently, scientists ~~which~~ *who/that* do biofuels research have been working to overcome these problems. For example, some scientists have produced a genetically modified tobacco that ~~it~~ contains more oil than usual. Other scientists have produced genetically modified tobacco plants that ~~they~~ produce a lot of oil. This oil can be made into ethanol. In fact, some scientists have produced ethanol from inedible grass that ~~it~~ grows in the wild. The scientists ~~which~~ *who/that* made these inventions hope that biofuels will become an important part of our renewable energy future.

6 Grammar for Writing
Using Subject Relative Clauses to Avoid Repetition

Pre-writing Task

1 page 294

Possible answers:
The writer promotes using reusable shopping bags because it is a very easy change to make to help the environment.

2 page 295

People everywhere are concerned with the future of our planet, (whose) environment is rapidly deteriorating. Environmentalists (who) want to help protect the planet are working hard to find environmentally sound alternatives (that) are also economical. However, there are many changes (that) are relatively easy to make. One change (that) could make a significant impact is using reusable bags instead of plastic or paper bags when shopping. Plastic bags, (which) might take up to 1,000 years to degrade, are very destructive for the environment. Between 500 billion to 1 trillion plastic bags are used each year around the world. In various parts of the world, laws (which) would stop the use of plastic bags entirely are being discussed or implemented. Paper bags are not as harmful for the environment as plastic, but they still cause a significant amount of damage. Approximately 14 million trees are cut down each year just to supply Americans with paper bags. In some stores in the United States, shoppers (who) use their own bags are given five cents back for each bag. However, even though using reusable shopping bags instead of plastic or paper is a very easy change to make, only a small minority of people in the United States have begun to do it voluntarily. In years to come, there will likely be laws that regulate the use of shopping bags to protect the environment.

Writing Task

1 Write page 295
Answers will vary.

2 Self-Edit page 295
Answers will vary.

22 Object Relative Clauses (Adjective Clauses with Object Relative Clauses)

Biometrics

1 Grammar in the Real World

A page 296

Answers will vary; Possible answers: Some modern techniques are fiber matching, scent dogs, fingerprinting, and face recognition.

B Comprehension Check page 297

Possible answers:
1. Some types of forensic evidence are dust, hair, and fibers.
2. One way that police can identify someone is through their fingerprints / through face recognition software.
3. Fiber matching can only match certain types of cloth, and scent dogs don't have strict training standards.

C Notice page 297
1. b   2. c   3. a
They function as objects.

2 Indentifying Object Relative Clauses

Exercise 2.1 Forming Identifying Object Relative Clauses pages 298–299

2. which; analyze
3. who; suspect
4. which; have
5. which; utilize
6. who; admit
7. which; uses

Exercise 2.2 Using Identifying Object Relative Clauses page 299

2. It's a hand-held device which/that officers bring to the crime scene.
3. It helps the police to analyze data which/that they find at the scene.
4. The device has privacy issues which/that some people are concerned about.
5. Well, the DNA which/that the device collected might get the person in trouble.
6. For example, many people have health issues which/that they want to keep private.

Exercise 2.3 Sentence Combining

A page 300

2. whom the police sent to the crime scene made their report

3. that the police recovered had been stolen
4. whose home burglars invaded has not been identified
5. have visited the house which the thief broke into yesterday
6. that a car hit last night is in good condition

B Pair Work page 300

1. X
2. The detectives the police sent to the crime scene made their report.
3. Several valuable items the police recovered had been stolen.
4. X
5. Detectives have visited the house the thief broke into yesterday.
6. The man a car hit last night is in good condition.

3 Nonrestrictive Object Relative Clauses

Exercise 3.1 Nonidentifying Object Relative Clauses page 301

Forensic science, <u>which many of you know about from popular TV shows</u>, has become a popular career. Forensic science courses, <u>which many colleges are offering today</u>, prepare students for careers in crime scene investigation. The University of Central Florida (UCF), <u>which I attended</u>, has a forensic science program. Your area of specialization, <u>which you choose during your time here</u>, depends on your interests and skills. The area that I chose was forensic biochemistry because I wanted to study odontology. Forensic odontology, <u>which the police use to analyze teeth</u>, is challenging and fascinating. Forensic analysis, <u>which focuses on chemistry and analysis of different kinds of evidence</u>, is also available. Introduction to Forensic Science, <u>which you take after other preliminary courses</u>, will help you decide on the area of specialty. I wish you all the best of luck!

Exercise 3.2 Using Nonidentifying Object Relative Clauses page 302

2. , which CBS first aired in 2000, was an immediate hit
3. , which the entertainment industry has awarded six Emmys, has been on the air for over 10 years
4. , which over 70 million people have watched, is shown around the world
5. , which Pete Townsend wrote in the 1970s, is the *CSI* theme song
6. , which CBS created on the same model as the original *CSI*, also had high ratings

4 Object Relative Clauses as Objects of Prepositions

Exercise 4.1 Prepositions and Object Relative Clauses

A pages 303–304

2. which; on
3. from which
4. who; with
5. that; with
6. which; in

B page 304

Same as **A**.

Exercise 4.2 Using Prepositions and Object Relative Clauses

A page 304

2. which/that/Ø the broken furniture was lying on
3. who/whom/that/Ø I spoke to
4. which/that/Ø the crime took place in
5. which/that/Ø the criminal entered through
6. which/that/Ø I sent the evidence to

B page 304

2. I found fibers on the floor on which the broken furniture was lying.
3. The neighbors to whom I spoke said they heard nothing.
4. The house in which the crime took place was unlocked.
5. There were fingerprints on the door through which the criminal entered.
6. The lab to which I sent the evidence matched the fingerprints immediately.

5 Avoid Common Mistakes

Editing Task page 305

A victim who police have taken ~~her~~ to the police station gives testimony. She looks at a man in a police lineup and says, "That's the person ~~which~~ I saw in my car." During the
who/whom/that/Ø
trial, the woman gives her testimony in front of the jury, and the jury makes a decision. Soon, the man goes to jail. However, it is possible the woman whose testimony was used is wrong. Researchers now claim that the eyewitness
that/which/Ø
stories ~~what~~ courts often rely on are not always reliable.

that/which
Psychologists have conducted experiments ~~who~~ revealed some surprising results. They played a crime-scene video for participants and then asked the participants to remember details. Results showed that participants often described events/which they knew nothing about and had not seen in the video. Similarly, the
who/whom/that/Ø
suspect ~~what~~ participants chose out of a police lineup was rarely the actual criminal.

Psychologists who courts have hired ~~them~~ have testified that eyewitness testimony is not as accurate as was once assumed. As such, psychologists have developed new rules to guide the use of eyewitness testimony.

6 Grammar for Writing

Using Object Relative Clauses to Provide Background Information

Pre-writing Task

1 page 306

Possible answers:
The Innocence Project helps innocent people who have been convicted of crimes they did not commit. It has helped almost 300 people since 1989.

2 page 307

The Innocence Project is a legal organization (whose) purpose is to free innocent people from prison. These people have been imprisoned for crimes (that) they did not commit. The Innocence Project was created in 1992 by two lawyers (who) knew about a famous study about how unreliable eyewitness reports could be. This study showed that it was important to find another way of proving a person's guilt or innocence, especially in the case of serious crimes. At that time, DNA testing was a relatively new process. The first time that DNA testing helped prove someone's innocence was in the 1980s in England. In this case, police arrested a man (who) had been accused of committing two serious crimes. However, the police were not convinced that they had the right man, so they hired a doctor (whose) specialty was working with DNA. The DNA testing (that) the doctor performed proved that the suspect was not guilty. The founders of the Innocence Project thought that DNA testing might help prove that some prisoners were innocent of the crimes for which they had been convicted. Since the Innocence Project was established, it has been very successful. DNA testing, with which most people are now very familiar, has been responsible for freeing almost 300 prisoners since 1989. *Nonidentifying clause:* lines 14–15: with which most people are now very familiar

Writing Task

1 Write page 307

Answers will vary.

2 Self-Edit page 307

Answers will vary.

23 Relative Clauses with *Where* and *When*; Reduced Relative Clauses

Millennials

1 Grammar in the Real World

A page 308

Answers will vary.

B Comprehension Check page 309

Possible answers:
1. Millennials were born in the 1980s and 1990s.
2. Millennials have such high self-confidence and expectations because they were raised at a time when parents and teachers believed in a lot of praising and rewarding.
3. They are good at technology-based jobs because they were raised in the era of computers, cell phones, and the Internet.

C Notice page 309

1. who is   2. who was
Subject relative clauses

2 Relative Clauses with *Where* and *When*

Exercise 2.1 Object Relative Clauses with *Where* and *When* page 311

2. in which   5. where
3. when   6. when
4. in which   7. Ø

Exercise 2.2 More Object Relative Clauses with *Where* and *When*

A page 311
2. b   3. a   4. b

B page 312
2. when   5. where
3. where   6 during which
4. in which   7. in which

C page 312
Same as **B**.

Exercise 2.3 Relative Clauses with *When*
page 313

Possible answers:
2. The year 1963 is the year when / in which / during which President Kennedy died.
3. The year 1975 is the year when / in which / during which the Vietnam War ended.
4. The years 1965–1981 are the years when / in which / during which the Gen Xers were born.
5. The year 1989 is the year when / in which / during which the Berlin Wall fell.
6. The years 1980–2000 are the years when / in which / during which the Millennials were born.
7. The year 2007 is the year when / in which / during which the Great Recession began.

3 Reduced Relative Clauses

Exercise 3.1 Reducing Relative Clauses

A pages 315–316
2. ☐
3. ☑
4. ☑
5. ☐
6. ☑
7. ☐
8. ☑
9. ☑
10. ☑
11. ☐

B page 316

3. Millennials in the workforce tend to have a "can-do" attitude.
4. Generation X, another large group in the workforce, does not tend to equate age with respect.
5. X
6. Baby Boomers, loyal employees, have started to retire from their jobs.
7. X
8. Baby Boomers graduating from college in the 1960s lived in prosperous times.
9. Most Millennials not attending school say they intend to go back.
10. Many Millennials in school also have jobs.
11. X

C Pair Work page 316

Possible answers:

3. prepositional phrase
4. appositive
5. Can't be reduced because it doesn't have a form of *be*
6. appositive
7. Can't be reduced because it's an object relative clause
8. participle phrase
9. participle phrase
10. prepositional phrase
11. Can't be reduced because it doesn't have a form of *be*

Exercise 3.2 Relative Clauses with *Be* + Prepositional Phrases and *Be* + Adjectives + Prepositional Phrases page 317

2. who are good with technology; People good with technology have an advantage here.
3. who are familiar with social networking; Workers familiar with social networking will be able to use these skills here.
4. who are good at multitasking; Employees good at multitasking will enjoy our fast-paced environment.
5. who are high in self-esteem; Employees high in self-esteem do well here.
6. who are interested in advancement; People interested in advancement will find it here.
7. who are in our training programs; Employees in our training programs appreciate learning new skills.
8. who are accustomed to a dynamic environment; People accustomed to a dynamic environment will be happy here.

Exercise 3.3 Relative Clauses with Adjectives page 318

2. X
3. Even confident Millennials appreciate feedback.
4. Millennials appreciate structured work environments.

5. X
6. It's important to provide challenges for bored Millennials.
7. Managers must not overwork family-oriented Millennials.
8. X
9. X
10. Unemployed Millennials don't always have a lot of experience in job interviews.

Exercise 3.4 Using Adjective Phrases

Pair Work page 318

Answers will vary.

4 Avoid Common Mistakes

Editing Task page 319

There was a time ~~in~~ when my mother always complained about my use of technology. She did not understand why I had to constantly text friends and go online. My mother, ~~is~~ a digital immigrant, grew up without a lot of tech gadgets. As a result, she is uncomfortable using technology at the office where ^she^ works. On the other hand, my brothers and I, ~~are~~ all digital natives, are happy to use technology all the time.

Digital natives, ~~are~~ lifelong technology users, use electronic devices instinctively. These people do not remember a time ~~in~~ when they were not connected to the Internet. In fact, they find it annoying when they go to places where ^they^ cannot connect to the Internet. Digital immigrants, in contrast, remember a time ~~in~~ when there was no Internet. As a result, some of them see the Internet as useful but not essential. In addition, digital immigrants sometimes find it difficult to figure out how to use technology. For example, when my mother first began uploading information, she had to call someone for help. Lately, however, my mother has found a social networking site where ^she^ often goes in her free time to stay in touch with friends and family members.

5 Grammar for Writing
Using Reduced Subject Relative Clauses to Make Ideas Clearer

Pre-writing Task

1 page 320

Possible answers:
Millennials are known for multitasking and teamwork.

2 page 321

Millennials, experts at multitasking, are the first generation to grow up in a digital age. Some people believe that in addition to making Millennials good at multitasking, this has also made them good at teamwork, a much valued skill in American workplaces. Because many U.S. Millennials had access to cell phones, computers, and social networks from their early teens, they grew up accustomed to having conversations with more than one person at a time, a common feature of texting and social networking. This ability to talk to more than one person at a time seems to have prepared Millennials for communicating successfully with several team members at once. Multitasking is a skill that they have mastered easily. In addition, the idea of waiting to talk to someone is a strange idea to this generation. Millennials, used to talking to people whenever they need to, don't wait to find a landline phone or to see someone in person in order to communicate. They tend to deal with things as they come up, rather than waiting until later. This can be a valuable quality because team members who get things done quickly help create a more efficient team. Perhaps because of these factors, smart employers are recruiting Millennials to build strong teams in their companies.

line 1: who are experts at multitasking
lines 3–4: which is a much valued skill in American
    workplaces
lines 6–7: which is a common feature of texting and social
    networking
line 11: who are used to talking to people whenever they
    need to

Writing Task

1 Write page 321

Answers will vary.

2 Self-Edit page 321

Answers will vary.

24 Real Conditionals: Present and Future
Media in the United States

1 Grammar in the Real World

A page 322

Answers will vary; Possible answer: The writer thinks that people tend to only read media that reflect their own views, which reinforces a biased view of issues.

B Comprehension Check page 323

Possible answers:
1. Some political analysts claim that Americans tend to read, watch, and listen to the news media that reflect their own views.
2. One example of this is when people who support the president's policies also choose to read online news pages with a similar view. These websites likely explain how the crisis was caused by politicians from the opposing party. So these people might be convinced that the crisis was the fault of the opposing party.
3. People might become even more isolated in their beliefs in the future because links in blogs and web pages will connect people with information that supports only their views.

C Notice page 323

1. present situation
2. future situation

2 Present Real Conditionals
Exercise 2.1 Present Real Conditionals for Habits and Routines page 324

"When I $\underset{(1)}{\underline{am}}$ in the car, I $\underset{(2)}{\underline{listen}}$ to the radio. My husband $\underset{(3)}{\underline{watches}}$ the comedy news shows if he $\underset{(4)}{\underline{stays}}$ up late."
– Alexa, 28, office manager.

"If a friend $\underset{(5)}{\underline{texts}}$ me about something interesting, I generally $\underset{(6)}{\underline{check}}$ out other websites to find out more information." – Su Ho, 32, engineer.

Exercise 2.2 Present Real Conditionals for Facts, General Truths, Habits, and Routines page 325

2. I hear about a good story, I try to go beyond the basic facts

3. I feel like I'm getting emotionally involved in a story,
   I drop it
4. Many people talk about it; a story is important
5. I move quickly; my editor calls and tells me to
   investigate a story

Exercise 2.3 Emphasizing the Result in Present Real Conditionals

A page 326

2. If a newspaper prints sensational headlines, then it probably isn't/is not accurate.
3. If a newspaper prints an important story in the back of the newspaper, then it probably isn't/is not balanced.
4. If a magazine prints an unflattering photo of a politician, then it's/it is probably biased.
5. If a reporter uses words with negative connotation instead of neutral terms, then he/she probably isn't/is not fair.

B Pair Work page 326

Answers will vary.

Exercise 2.4 Present Real Conditionals

A Over to You page 327

Answers will vary.

B Pair Work page 327

Answers will vary.

3 Future Real Conditionals

Exercise 3.1 Future Real Conditionals for Predictions page 328

2. You will be a better critical thinker if you listen to opposing viewpoints.
3. You will become a more informed voter if you understand the issues.
4. You will make better choices in future elections if you learn about the candidates' voting records.
5. If a person learns about economics, he will make wiser financial decisions.
6. If people get the news from several sources, they will have a more complete picture of an issue.

Exercise 3.2 Future Real Conditionals for Predictions and Plans

A page 329

Possible answers:

2. If we stop home deliveries, we'll lose money.
3. If we charge for online access, we'll increase revenue.

4. If we don't find new advertisers, we won't make more money.
5. If we put more articles online, we'll attract new readers.

B page 329

2. a		5. b
3. a		6. a
4. b		

Exercise 3.3 Future Real Conditionals with More than One Result

Over to You page 330

Answers will vary.

4 Real Conditionals with Modals, Modal-like Expressions, and Imperatives

Exercise 4.1 Real Conditionals with Modals and Modal-like Expressions page 331

2. you should do it today
3. you ought to volunteer
4. can tutor children
5. you have to watch the news
6. they might influence the outcome
7. you could change things
8. shouldn't/should not complain

Exercise 4.2 Real Conditionals with Imperatives

Pair Work page 331

Answers will vary.

Exercise 4.3 Real Conditionals with Modals, Modal-like Expressions, and Imperatives

A page 332

Action	Do	Don't
2.	✓	
3.	✓	
4.		✓
5.		✓
6.		✓

B page 332

2. want; visit
3. want; must; visit
4. Do not rely on; want
5. Don't pay; want
6. don't let; want

5 Avoid Common Mistakes

Editing Task page 333

    If incoming students want to learn what this college
is like, where ⌃they ~~should~~ look? If they visit the college
should

website ⌄, they can learn about sports and campus events.

However, incoming freshmen might want a more personal

perspective. They may not have the time to attend lectures

and other events, or they may want some anonymity. I have

decided to start a blog that provides an alternative source

of information and help.

    ~~When~~ I want the blog to be successful at helping
If

students, I will need to provide practical suggestions. For

example, one concern may be, "If I want to meet people

with similar interests, what ⌃I ~~can~~ do?" I will tell that person
can

places where he or she can post requests on the school

website and how to write his or her requests. I will also

include ways to safely respond to queries.

    In addition, if a student ~~will have~~ a problem with
has

a teacher, I will write about it in my blog and provide

possible ways to solve it. If people want to add advice,

how ⌃they ~~can~~ do so? They can share advice by commenting.
can

If professors want to comment, they can, too.

    I will not try to write like a journalist and give a lot of

facts. If students ~~will~~ want facts, they can go to the college

website. In contrast, I will give them personal advice that

will help them with everyday problems. If students want

real answers to their problems ⌄,they should try my blog.

6 Grammar for Writing

Using a Single *If* Clause with Multiple Main Clauses

Pre-writing Task

1 page 334

Possible answers:
The problem the writer is concerned about is choosing
movies. The writer suggests finding reviewers you agree
with and reading their reviews.

2 page 335

    It is the weekend and you want to see a movie. How
do you choose which movie to see? (If you are like some
people,) you choose movies based on the actors that are in
them. However, <u>if that is how you choose</u>, <u>you probably are
not always happy with your movie choice.</u> <u>You probably
end up wasting your money sometimes on forgettable
movies or even on movies that put you to sleep.</u> Many
moviegoers choose movies based on their previews and
TV advertisements. However, trusting these sources is
another ineffective way to choose movies because previews
and ads are expertly created to make even the worst movie
look like an award-winning film. You are more likely to be
happy with your choices (if you read movie reviews before
choosing movies). However, even reading movie reviews
can cause problems. You might not agree with the
reviewer. <u>If you want to minimize your chances of being
disappointed with your movie choice</u>, <u>read more than one
movie critic's review.</u> <u>Choose your reviewers carefully.</u> <u>Find
reviewers with whom you almost always agree.</u> (If you use
the Internet for finding movie times and locations), use it
to read reviews of movies you loved, too. (When you find
reviewers that like the same movies you like), return to
those reviewers' websites when choosing a movie to see.
This technique will not guarantee that you will love every
movie that you choose from now on, but you probably will
not fall asleep at the next movie you see.
Answers will vary.

Writing Task

1 Write page 335
Answers will vary.

2 Self-Edit page 335
Answers will vary.

25 Unreal Conditionals: Present, Future, and Past
Natural Disasters

1 Grammar in the Real World

A page 336

Answers will vary; Possible answer: One positive effect of Hurricane Katrina is that it provided a fresh start to rebuild the city's schools.

B Comprehension Check page 337

Possible answers:
1. It killed over 1,800 people and caused over $75 billion in damages.
2. He hired top teachers, modernized classrooms, and started several charter schools.
3. Charter schools are independently run public schools.

C Notice page 337

1. If they found a strong school superintendent, <u>they could hope for real change.</u>
2. If you had been a public school student in New Orleans prior to 2005, <u>you would have had little hope for the future of your education.</u>
3. Vallas knew that if state exam scores improved, <u>the charter schools would be considered a success.</u>
4. If Katrina hadn't happened, <u>the school might have been closed down.</u>

The situations are imaginary.

2 Present and Future Unreal Conditionals

Exercise 2.1 Present and Future Unreal Conditionals page 339

3. we might need earthquake insurance
4. If there weren't/were not a tsunami warning *OR* If there wasn't/was not a tsunami warning
5. we would be prepared for an earthquake
6. If there weren't/were not a tornado warning *OR* If there wasn't/was not a tornado warning
7. we might not have to leave the building
8. If everyone weren't/were not worrying about the storm

Exercise 2.2 Present and Future Unreal Conditionals: Imagined Possibilities
pages 339–340

2. could build; would be
3. couldn't/could not build; would suffer
4. could avoid; wouldn't/would not get
5. could improve; would be

Exercise 2.3 Present and Future Unreal Conditionals: Predicted Results

A Over to You page 340

Answers will vary.

B Group Work page 340

Answers will vary.

Exercise 2.4 *If I Were You . . .* for Advice

A page 341

2. If I were you, I'd/I would get earthquake insurance.
3. If I were you, I'd/I would not go to work. *OR* If I were you, I'd/I would stay indoors.
4. If I were you, I'd/I would stay indoors. *OR* If I were you, I'd/I would not go to work.
5. If I were you, I'd/I would leave immediately. *OR* If I were you, I'd/I would leave the building.
6. If I were you, I'd/I would leave the building. *OR* If I were you, I'd/I would leave immediately.

B Pair Work page 341

No answers.

3 Past Unreal Conditionals

Exercise 3.1 Past Unreal Conditionals
pages 342–343

3. would have survived
4. hadn't/had not exploded
5. hadn't/had not covered
6. wouldn't/would not have been preserved
7. would have stayed
8. hadn't/had not changed
9. hadn't/had not been
10. wouldn't/would not have known

Exercise 3.2 Past Unreal Conditionals: Regret

A Group Work page 343

Answers will vary.

B page 344

2. F   5. T
3. F   6. T
4. T   7. F

C page 344

Same as **A.**

D page 344

2. could/might have hit
3. would have survived
4. could/might have affected

5. wouldn't/would not have done
6. wouldn't/would not have seen
7. wouldn't/would not have learned

4 Wishes About the Present, Future, and Past

Exercise 4.1 Present and Future Wishes
page 346

2. wish (that) we had enough bottled water
3. wishes (that) the roof wasn't/was not leaking
4. wishes (that) we weren't/were not running out of batteries
5. wishes (that) the electricity worked
6. wishes (that) the Internet was/were working
7. wish (that) the furniture wasn't/weren't/was not/were not going to be ruined
8. wish (that) we could go to a hotel

Exercise 4.2 Past Wishes page 346

Possible answers:
2. I wish (that) they hadn't/had not closed the beach. *OR* I wish (that) they had let people in to clean it up.
3. I wish (that) a flood hadn't destroyed the city. *OR* I wish (that) there had been records.
4. I wish (that) a hurricane hadn't destroyed my high school. *OR* I wish (that) we had been able to attend graduation.

5 Avoid Common Mistakes

Editing Task page 347

If Hurricane Ike ~~did~~ _had_ not come, we would have had an easier time. If the storm _had_ missed us, we would not have lived without electricity for two weeks. We would have been able to go to work and school. Our trees would look a lot better if _they_ had not been destroyed by the strong winds. For these reasons, some people wish that Hurricane Ike _had_ never happened. However, I do not. If the storm ~~did~~ _had_ not come to Houston, we would not have learned many valuable lessons.

First, we learned about our neighbors. We all came together to help each other before and after the storm. If I ~~live~~ _had lived_ in a different place, maybe I would not have gotten to know my neighbors in this way. Second, we learned good emergency survival skills. If we had not learned to board our houses, _they_ might have been damaged. If another storm ~~comes~~ _came_ today, my house would be safe.

Sometimes I wish that my family ~~did not move~~ _hadn't/had not moved_ to this city. However, I do not feel this way because of the hurricanes. The hurricanes have made our community stronger.

6 Grammar for Writing

Using *If* Clauses to Support Ideas

Pre-writing Task

1 page 348

Possible answers:
The writer's family should have created an escape plan and should have made a list of important things.

2 page 349

Every family should have an escape plan in case of a house fire, but California families need escape plans for wildfires as well. My family discovered this last year. A wildfire began several miles away from our house on a Sunday afternoon. By Tuesday, it was very close. We didn't have an escape plan because we were new to California. At the time, we did not know about the dangers of wildfires. <u>If we had lived in California longer, we would have thought about wildfire preparation more carefully.</u> At 7:00 that evening, the police called to tell us that our area was in a warning zone. They told us that we should start getting prepared to leave. My children and I started packing up our belongings. We also thought about where to go. We decided that we would go to a friend's house. <u>We could not have brought our pets if we had gone to the emergency shelter.</u> By 8:30, the wildfire had started moving faster, and we got the call that we had to evacuate. We had not finished packing, but we put the animals in the car and left. Two days later, we were able to return to our home. We were lucky because our house was fine. When we looked around, we realized we had taken silly things and left important things. <u>If our house had burned down, we could have lost many important papers.</u> We decided that we had to make a list of important things immediately in case of another fire. <u>We would not have panicked as much, and we might have packed better, if we had made that list before the fire. Next time, we will be prepared.</u>

The modals *could* and *might* are also used in the main clauses.

Writing Task

1 Write page 349

Answers will vary.

2 Self-Edit page 349

Answers will vary.

26 Conjunctions
Globalization of Food

1 Grammar in the Real World

A page 350

Answers will vary; Possible answer: To make customers happy, fast-food businesses serve both food from their U.S. menus and food adapted to the tastes and customs of local cultures.

B Comprehension Check page 351

Possible answers:

1. To succeed globally, Dunkin' Donuts thinks globally but acts locally.
2. To attract vegetarians in India, McDonald's offers only vegetarian burgers and prepares non-vegetarian meals separately.
3. The United States is affected by the globalization of fast food because fast-food restaurants from other countries have spread globally into the United States.

C Notice page 351

1. but; b
2. not only; but also; b
3. and; a

2 Connecting Words and Phrases with Conjunctions

Exercise 2.1 Coordinating Conjunctions
page 353

Possible answers:

2. Starbucks operates in Asia, Europe, and Latin America.
3. The U.S. branch doesn't have vegetarian burgers or lamb burgers.
4. Would you prefer to try something unusual or familiar?
5. Vegans don't eat eggs, cheese, or yogurt.
6. The food is cheap but very healthy.
7. The coffee is expensive but very popular.

Exercise 2.2 Correlative Conjunctions

A page 354

2. either; or
3. neither; nor
4. Not only; but also
5. Neither; nor
6. either; or
7. Both; and
8. not only; but also

B Group Work page 355

Answers will vary.

Exercise 2.3 More Correlative Conjunctions page 355

Possible answers:

2. Tea is both inexpensive and very popular in Egypt.
3. You can use either your own mug or a store cup at coffee shops in the U.K.
4. Not only donuts but also muffins are available in the United States.
5. Not only recycling but also reusing cups is encouraged in China.
6. Generally, neither forks nor knives are available in Chinese restaurants.
7. Neither hot dogs nor pizza is typically eaten for lunch in the Dominican Republic.

3 Connecting Sentences with Coordinating Conjunctions

Exercise 3.1 Connecting Sentences with *And, But, Or* pages 357–358

2. First, they studied the new market, <u>and</u> they even sent anthropologists to study U.S. eating and shopping habits.
3. They opened stores in wealthy neighborhoods, <u>and</u> they also opened some in low-income neighborhoods.
4. The trend in the United States is toward "big box" stores, <u>but</u> FoodCo decided to open small, convenience-type stores.
5. Convenience stores in the United States usually do not sell fresh produce, <u>but</u> FoodCo has changed the definition of convenience store with its new stores.
6. FoodCo has positioned itself as a healthy convenience store, <u>and</u> it provides high-quality groceries and produce at reasonable prices.
7. Customers can use FoodCo's shops to pick up last-minute items, <u>or</u> they can do their weekly shopping there.
8. Now shoppers in low-income neighborhoods have a choice. They can buy junk food at a convenience store, <u>but/or</u> they can buy healthy products at a FoodCo shop.

Exercise 3.2 Connecting Sentences with *So* and *Yet* page 358

2. , yet   6. , so
3. , yet   7. , so
4. , so   8. , yet
5. , yet

Exercise 3.3 Combining Sentences page 359

2. I have eaten tacos in China and ordered kimchi in France.
3. You might get an authentic dish abroad or find a local version of it.
4. I often find international dishes abroad, but they are usually adapted to local tastes.
5. Beef isn't eaten in some countries, so a fast-food chain might sell lamb burgers.
6. I travel constantly, yet I never miss food from home.

Exercise 3.4 Using *So* and *Yet*

Over to You page 359

Answers will vary.

4 Reducing Sentences with Similar Clauses

Exercise 4.1 Reducing Sentences with Similar Clauses page 361

2. Some U.S. food companies are successful in India, but some (U.S. food companies) aren't.
3. Beef isn't popular in India, and neither is pork.; Beef isn't popular in India, and pork isn't either.
4. McDonald's adapts its menu to local tastes, and so does Pizza Hut.; McDonald's adapts its menu to local tastes, and Pizza Hut does, too.
5. Pizza Hut doesn't serve meat in some regions, and neither does McDonalds.; Pizza Hut doesn't serve meat in some regions, and McDonald's doesn't, either.

Exercise 4.2 Reducing Verb Forms

A Group Work page 362

2. e   4. a
3. d   5. c

B page 362

2. F
3. T
4. F

C pages 362–363

2. but eel hasn't
3. and sea urchin didn't, either
4. and so have cold noodles
5. and our other restaurants can't, either
6. and the other branches will, too
7. and most other Asian restaurants won't, either
8. and the cake has, too

5 Avoid Common Mistakes

Editing Task page 363

My roommate and I come from different cultures,
        both
so ~~either~~ our eating habits and food preferences differ.

Fortunately, we have some food preferences in common.
                          either
I do not eat junk food, and he does not, ~~too~~. There are no
        or
cookies ~~and~~ other desserts in our house. Instead, we have
both
~~either~~ fresh fruits and nuts for snacks.

                                    both
    However, we have some differences. I eat ~~either~~ rice and
pasta every day. My roommate, however, thinks meals with
rice/and dishes with pasta will make him gain weight, so
he does not want to eat them often. Likewise, I do not like
                        or
to eat a lot of meat ~~and~~ dairy products because I believe
they are not healthy. Fortunately, I do not complain about
                              either
his tastes, and he does not complain about mine, ~~too~~.
                                  both
When we cook, we try to make food that represents ~~either~~
his culture and mine.

6 Grammar for Writing

Using Coordinating and Correlative Conjunctions to Join Words and Clauses

Pre-writing Task

1 page 364

Possible answers:
One difference is that Mexican food does not use sour cream, while Tex-Mex food does.

2 page 365

Mexican food can be found in most parts of the United States, <u>but</u> Americans will probably be very surprised on their first trip to Mexico. U.S. visitors to Mexico are unlikely to find many of the foods they usually order in their favorite

Mexican restaurants. For example, they will find neither nachos nor chimichangas, which are foods commonly found in typical Mexican restaurants in the United States. That's because these dishes are either American foods that were influenced by Mexican foods or Mexican dishes that were combined with American dishes. A common U.S. variation of Mexican food is the addition of sour cream and cheese to many dishes. Mexicans sometimes use a little bit of something similar to sour cream or sprinkle some cheese on their dishes, but they do not use much. Many of these Mexican-influenced American dishes originated in Texas near the Mexican border and then spread throughout the United States. This is where the term "Tex-Mex" came from.

Writing Task

1 Write page 365

Answers will vary.

2 Self-Edit page 365

Answers will vary.

27 Adverb Clauses and Phrases
Consumerism

1 Grammar in the Real World

A page 366

Answers will vary; Possible answer: Shopping is an addiction when someone is unable to control spending.

B Comprehension Check page 367

Possible answers:
1. Shopping addictions aren't considered a serious problem by most people because shopping is viewed as an amusing addiction.
2. Shopping addiction can lead to feelings of depression or guilt after a shopping trip. Also, shopaholics might have financial problems. Shopping addiction can also lead to lies which may destroy families.
3. Shopaholics can treat their problem by admitting they have a problem and getting help or by taking a friend with them when they go shopping.

C Notice page 367

1. Even though; a
2. Because; b
3. Even though; a

2 Subordinators and Adverb Clauses
Exercise 2.1 Adverb Clauses page 369

2. Many people feel that it is patriotic to shop because some politicians say that it is good for the economy.
3. Even though we may not need items, we sometimes want what others have.
4. Although shopping addiction seems to be a recent problem, it has almost certainly existed for centuries.
5. While addicts may shop to escape negative feelings, normal people shop to buy things they need. *OR* Addicts may shop to escape negative feelings, while normal people shop to buy things they need.
6. While normal shoppers use the items they buy, compulsive shoppers often do not use them. *OR* Normal shoppers use the items they buy, while compulsive shoppers often do not use them.

Exercise 2.2 More Adverb Clauses

A page 370

2. Because my insurance pays for it, I was able to sign up for therapy.
3. Although I've only been in therapy a short time, I'm feeling better already.
4. Since I only buy what I really need, I'm spending much less money.
5. Even though I was at the mall yesterday, I only went to one store.
6. Since I had a list, I only bought things I truly needed.

B page 370

Same as **A**.

Exercise 2.3 Using Adverb Clauses

Group Work page 370

Answers will vary.

3 Reducing Adverb Clauses
Exercise 3.1 Reducing Clauses That Give Reasons page 372

2. Understanding that he had a problem
3. Having spent so much money on clothes
4. Having received treatment
5. Having worked with a therapist
6. Having gotten help

Exercise 3.2 Reducing Time Clauses

page 372

2. While spending money
3. before getting treatment
4. Before spending more money
5. After joining DA
6. after starting DA
7. since receiving treatment

4 Subordinators to Express Purpose

Exercise 4.1 Using Subordinators to Express Purpose

A page 373

2. Some people buy things *to* feel good about themselves.

3. Some people acquire things *so that* they have a sense of who they are.

4. It's also possible that people acquire things *in order to* feel secure.

5. They buy a lot *in order to* feel that they are financially secure.

6. They buy a lot *so that* they are prepared for any emergency.

7. ~~Find~~ *To find* out how little you really need, think about what you would do if you had to move.

8. I think that *in order to* have true peace of mind, you should have as little as possible.

B Group Work page 374

Answers will vary.

C page 374

Answers will vary.

5 Avoid Common Mistakes

Editing Task page 375

After ~~look~~ *looking* at research, we see clearly that alcohol and drug addictions are serious physical conditions. Psychologists are now considering adding shopping to the list. ~~Eventhough~~ *Even though* these experts say that shopping is as addictive as drugs, I disagree that it should be considered a serious addiction.

People who argue that shopping is addictive have good reasons. While ~~shop~~ *shopping*, many people get a good feeling. They like spending money ~~even~~ *even though* they may not need to buy anything. However, after ~~go~~ *going* home, they feel regret. They have spent money on something they did not want or ~~need.~~ *need because* ~~Because~~ buying something makes them feel a sense of power.

However, after ~~examine~~ the situation of over-shopping closely, one can see that many people are victims of advertising. ~~Even~~ *Even though* they may not plan to buy something, a powerful advertisement can change their mind. If people did not watch so much TV, they would not feel the urge to shop as strongly. In this way, shopping addiction differs from drug and alcohol addictions, which create a chemical change in the body that is very difficult to resist. ~~Eventhough~~ *Even though* shopping too much is a serious problem, it should not be considered an addiction. If advertisements disappeared, society would not have this problem called shopping addiction.

6 Grammar for Writing

Using Adverb Clauses to Give More Information About Main Clauses

Pre-writing Task

1 pages 376–377

Possible answers:
You don't need money because you buy things by giving away something else, not by paying with money.

2 page 377

<u>Although shopping usually requires money</u>, it has not always, and it does not have to now. In the past, <u>instead of paying for things that they needed with money</u>, people swapped skills and homemade items <u>so that they could "buy" the things they wanted or needed</u>. For example, a baker might trade freshly baked bread for coal or wood for the bakery oven. This was called bartering, and it used

to be done between neighbors and friends. The Internet has helped bring back this form of shopping, but this time with a modern twist. ✓ <u>Since the Internet is worldwide</u>, it is no longer necessary to find someone in your community to barter with. Now, you can barter with people all over the world. Bartering on the Internet not only saves people money but also solves the problem of how to get rid of unwanted things without creating more garbage. <u>Instead of throwing things away</u>, you can find homes for the things you no longer want or need. ✓ <u>Because there are so many websites that make this an easy thing to do</u>, more and more people are participating. Some websites require a token membership fee of a dollar or two, <u>while others simply require that you have something to give away before you can "buy" something for yourself</u>. Anyone can do this, provided that they can afford postage to send the things they are giving away. <u>After you have made a bartering agreement with someone</u>, all you have to do is sit back and wait for the things you have ordered to arrive. Internet bartering sites have made shopping both easy and painless, and they could even be helpful for shopaholics.

Writing Task

1 Write page 377

Answers will vary.

2 Self-Edit page 377

Answers will vary.

28 Connecting Information with Prepositions and Transitions
Technology in Entertainment

1 Grammar in the Real World

A page 378

Answers will vary; Possible answer: It has made the video games more realistic looking.

B Comprehension Check page 379

Possible answers:
1. Mocap is short for motion capture, which is the use of sensors to record movements.
2. Mocap is used in video games, movies, medicine, and job training.
3. Mocap isn't used more often because it's expensive, and it can't capture every motion.

C Notice page 379

1. b
2. a
3. c

2 Connecting Information with Prepositions and Prepositional Phrases
Exercise 2.1 Prepositional Phrases to Connect Ideas page 381

2. Due to / Because of
3. In addition to / As well as
4. instead of
5. as well as / in addition to
6. Because of / Due to

Exercise 2.2 More Prepositional Phrases to Connect Ideas page 381

2. As a result of
3. because of
4. besides

5. instead of
6. due to
7. Despite

Exercise 2.3 Using Prepositional Phrases to Connect Ideas

A page 382

2. Due to quick access to your records, doctors can share information with each other more easily.
3. In spite of many advantages to electronic records, some doctors still have serious concerns.
4. Instead of accurate information in the records, the information could contain data input errors.
5. Despite a lot of security, hackers could still steal information from hospitals.

B Group Work page 382

Answers will vary.

3 Connecting Information with Transition Words

Exercise 3.1 Transition Words to Show Sequence

A Pair Work page 384

a. 4   d. 3
b. 6   e. 2
c. 1   f. 5

B page 384

Same as **A**.

C page 385

2. Second, 5. After that,
3. Next,   6. Finally,
4. Then

Exercise 3.2 Transition Words for Academic Writing page 385

2. First   5. In contrast
3. Instead 6. In conclusion
4. Furthermore 7. therefore

Exercise 3.3 Using Transition Words

A page 386

2. *War of the Aliens* has excellent computer graphics. However, it has a dull plot.
3. Furthermore, *War of the Aliens* has unappealing characters.
4. On the other hand, *The Magical Forest* has an interesting story.
5. In addition, *The Magical Forest* has likeable characters.
6. Moreover, *The Magical Forest* has good dialog.
7. In contrast, *War of the Aliens* has bad dialog.
8. In conclusion, *The Magical Forest* is a better movie than *War of the Aliens.*

B Over to You page 386

Answers will vary.

4 Avoid Common Mistakes

Editing Task page 387

          the slow economy
Filmmaking is a durable industry. Despite ~~the economy is slow~~, the movie industry is doing well. People always seem to find money for entertainment. As a result, movie production companies often hire people because it takes many professionals to create a movie. In addition to ~~they~~ *hiring*

hire actors and directors, they hire tens of thousands of other professionals that are not well known – for example, grips (people who set up and tear down the sets), production assistants, and camera operators. The jobs can be exciting and challenging; ~~in~~ *on* the other hand, some can be low paying. As with most other careers, it is necessary to work hard and be ambitious to succeed. The work can also be especially tough for production crews – for example, camera operators, production assistants, and makeup artists – who work up to 18 hours a day. Despite ~~they have~~ *having* long hours, these jobs can be difficult to find because there is a lot of competition for them. In general, moviemaking is seen as a glamorous profession, and some people want to be a part of that glamour more than anything else. Movies require celebrities and artists; ~~in~~ *on* the other hand, they also rely on many people with other skills. It is a growing industry, too. The Bureau of Labor Statistics states that employment opportunities for people in the filmmaking industry will increase 14 percent between 2008 and 2018. In short, this industry is competitive, but young people should pursue it if they have an interest in movies.

5 Grammar for Writing

Using Prepositions and Transition Words to Support an Argument

Pre-writing Task

1 page 388

Possible answer:
The writer believes that 3D technology should be primarily used for animated or science-fiction movies.

2 page 389

  Movies that are in 3D can be a lot of fun and are becoming much more common. (However,) the technology should not be used too much because it is not good for all types of movies. (First,) 3D technology can be good for adventure, science fiction, and animated movies. (However,) it does not seem to work well for serious dramas and art films, where the plot and the characters are very important. (Instead of) getting involved in the plot and the characters, people tend to watch the special effects of the 3D technology when they watch a 3D movie. (As a result), the plot and characters fade in importance. (Thus), the 3D technology distracts the audience from the more important elements of the movie. (Second), many people cannot watch 3D movies for health reasons. Some people cannot physically see 3D technology (because of) an eye problem. There are others who get headaches or feel nauseated when they watch 3D movies. (Third), tickets for 3D movies are more expensive than tickets for regular movies. If more movies are made with 3D technology, people who do not want to spend a lot of money may have fewer movie choices. (As a result), people may go out to the movies less often. If moviemakers start making more 3D movies, they will be making movies that entertain only rather than enrich, which will be a terrible loss for the art of moviemaking. (In conclusion), I hope that 3D technology is used primarily for animated or science-fiction movies, and not for all types of movies.

Writing Task

1 Write   page 389

Answers will vary.

2 Self-Edit   page 389

Answers will vary.

Unit Tests with Answer Key

A ready-made Unit Test for each of the 28 units of the Student's Book is provided. The tests are easily scored, using a system found at the beginning of the Answer Key. Each test is available in both pdf and Microsoft Word formats.

Instructional PowerPoint® Presentations

The PowerPoint® presentations offer unit-specific grammar lessons for classroom use. The presentations include interactive versions of the *Grammar Presentations* for each unit.

CD-ROM Terms and Conditions of Use

This is a legal agreement between you ("the customer") and Cambridge University Press ("the publisher") for the *Grammar and Beyond 3 Teacher Support Resource CD-ROM*.

1. **Limited license**
   (a) You are purchasing only the right to use the CD-ROM and are acquiring no rights, express or implied, to the software itself, or the enclosed copy, other than those rights granted in this limited license for educational use only.
   (b) The publisher grants you the license to use one copy of this CD-ROM on your site and to install and use the software on this CD-ROM on a single computer. You may not install the software on this CD-ROM on a single secure network server for access from one site.
   (c) You shall not: (i) copy or authorize copying of the CD-ROM, (ii) translate the CD-ROM, (iii) reverse-engineer, alter, adapt, disassemble, or decompile the CD-ROM, (iv) transfer, sell, lease, lend, profit from, assign, or otherwise convey all or any portion of the CD-ROM, or (v) operate the CD-ROM from a mainframe system.

2. **Copyright**
   All titles and material contained within the CD-ROM are protected by copyright and all other applicable intellectual property laws, and international treaties. Therefore, you may not copy the CD-ROM. You may not alter, remove, or destroy any copyright notice or other material placed on or with this CD-ROM.

3. **Liability**
   The CD-ROM is supplied "as-is" with no express guarantee as to its suitability. To the extent permitted by applicable law, the publisher is not liable for costs of procurement of substitute products, damages, or losses of any kind whatsoever resulting from the use of this product, or errors or faults in the CD-ROM, and in every case the publisher's liability shall be limited to the suggested list price or the amount actually paid by the customer for the product, whichever is lower.

4. **Termination**
   Without prejudice to any other rights, the publisher may terminate this license if you fail to comply with the terms and conditions of the license. In such event, you must destroy all copies of the CD-ROM.

5. **Governing law**
   This agreement is governed by the laws of England, without regard to its conflict of laws provision, and each party irrevocably submits to the exclusive jurisdiction of the courts of England. The parties disclaim the application of the United Nations Convention on the International Sale of Goods.